INVESTIGATING LITERACY

INVESTIGATING LITERACY

A Sourcebook for Instruction with Adults

Colin J. Laine and Sue Geddis
University of Western Ontario

THOMPSON EDUCATIONAL PUBLISHING, INC.

1997

Thompson Educational Publishing, Inc.
11 Briarcroft Road, Toronto
Ontario, Canada M6S 1H3
Tel. (416) 766–2763 Fax (416) 766–0398

Canadian Cataloguing in Publication

Laine, Colin J.
Investigating literacy

Includes bibliographical references and index.
ISBN 1-55077-038-1

l. Literacy. 2. Elementary education of adults.
I. Geddis, Sue. II. Title.

LC5225.R4L35 1992 374'.012 C92-093849-3

Printed in Canada.
1 2 3 94 93 92

TABLE OF CONTENTS

PREFACE

This sourcebook has been written for the practitioner working with low-functioning adults and is designed to provide practitioners with sources of facts, ideas and resources that will enable them quickly to expand their skills.

An abundance of words has been written about learning styles, basic education for adults, literacy, adults considered illiterate and literacy programs. Where does one go to find appropriate help, and what do we really know for sure? Over the past decade, educators increasingly have understood that students approach various learning tasks in equally various and individualized ways which reflect particular and personalized learning styles. There are students, instructors and administrators whose style will be successful in some environments but not in others. Therefore, it is important to match personal styles to learning demands wherever possible. While the topic of learning styles has been written about and appropriate instruction has been initiated for children, little is known about relating knowledge of learning style to the instruction of adults.

Second, attention to literacy and its presumed impact on the social and economic welfare of Canada has intensified over the past five years. However, there is no general agreement on what literacy is or what "being literate" means. Much of the popular writing portrays the illiterate adult as incapable and credits illiteracy (in Canada) for poverty, disease, and unemployment. It is a widely held myth that illiteracy is increasing in North America and around the world: compared to what? For all that has been written, there is little or no evidence to prove the general claims.

If we appreciate and identify the predominant approaches or styles of learning in adults considered illiterate, then instructors can consider them in planning classroom instruction and materials. In this way, we hope that our clients will find the rewards and freedom that being literate brings.

Colin J. Laine
University of Western Ontario

ACKNOWLEDGMENTS

This book is one of the outcomes of the Literacy and Learning Styles Project, funded by the Social Sciences and Humanities Research Council of Canada and conducted by the Faculty of Education, The University of Western Ontario, London, Ontario. The development of the project is the result of the hard work and initiative of members of the Research Team and the generous co-operation of Ontario Basic Skills programs at Fanshawe College, London, Fanshawe College, St. Thomas, Lambton College, Sarnia, and Mohawk College, Hamilton.

This sourcebook has evolved from the initial searches by, and discussions with, my first research assistant, Terry Maier. I am particularly indebted to my primary assistant, Sue Geddis. Without her dedication, we may not have realized this goal. Sue collected and collated the materials, and her efforts in researching, designing and preparing the draft manuscript over many months have resulted in a work we believe will be of considerable benefit to anyone working in the field of literacy. I am indebted also to Linda Lysynchuk, my other research assistant, for her ongoing assistance and advice in the development of this manuscript.

A special thank-you goes to the students whose co-operation, interest, and desire continually encourage us, surprise us, and humble me.

Colin J. Laine, Director
Literacy/Learning Styles Project
London, Ontario

CO-AUTHOR'S ACKNOWLEDGMENTS

This bibliography is the result of Dr. Colin Laine's ability to create an atmosphere of learning and development which makes the unthinkable, thinkable. Although he was often behind the scenes of the project, he was, at the same time, always present with suggestions for making the finished product more comprehensive. I deeply appreciate his vision of our combined involvement in the work and for understanding how important it is for research assistants to have "real" involvement in research and not just be peripheral to the excitement.

I also recognize the important role of my co-researcher, Linda Lysynchuk, who took valuable time to discuss ideas with me. Her editorial readings of the initial product were very helpful in the revisions. She continues to be of great help in crystallizing my ideas and suggesting other areas that I could investigate profitably.

The library staff at the University of Western Ontario, Faculty of Education, has put up with a lot. They were cheerful, patient and always helpful in my search for the ultimate reference.

Susan Geddis
London, Ontario

1

INTRODUCTION

This sourcebook has been written for practitioners working with adults who are low-functioning or considered illiterate. It is designed to provide you with sources of facts, ideas and resources that will enable you and your students to expand your skills efficiently. The book is laid out in four, easily accessible, distinct sections which connect to provide a picture of the evolution of the Literacy/Learning Styles project.

The introduction overviews the book and the project; the succeeding chapters cover:

- Adult Education and Literacy (theoretical background);
- Assessment and Analysis, which considers the importance of learning styles and their assessment;
- Practice, which describes curricula, instructional strategies, teacher materials, alternative learning environments, and technology in the classroom; and,
- Future Directions and Resources, which provides the reader with ideas for the future and with literacy organizations, addresses of journals and newsletters, and lists publishers that carry materials in this area of adult education.

Each section begins with a brief overview of facts and ideas affecting learning and teaching for adults that we have found highlighted consistently in the literature. Each overview is followed by a selection of information sources: articles, books, materials, organizations and publications.

Several problems have arisen in investigating literacy and the programs designed for illiterate adults. First, there are a variety of eligibility criteria. There is ample evidence to show that the amount of schooling directly relates to a person's ability to read and to the richness of vocabulary (cf. Jones, Satin, Kelly, Montigny, 1990; Kirsch and Guthrie, 1981, 1987). The basic entry requirement to community college-based programs currently is a formal schooling of less than grade 8. Still, we have found the grade 8 requirement often has been ignored in the drive to gain more funding to cover the costs of the programs which are directly related to enrolment. Further, community programs have entry requirements from less than grade 5 up to less than grade 10 (National Literacy Secretariat, 1989).

Second, it is difficult to decide which abilities distinguish those adults considered illiterate from those who have English as a second language from those who have poor language or reading abilities, or from those who may have a learning disability. Many programs have broad, unreliable, or inconsistent, identification procedures that result in classes with adults who may have very different needs, abilities and goals. Further, we found few agencies complete any standardized or diagnostic assessments of entrants that translate to instructional strategies or that give teachers an understanding of their clients' specific learning needs.

Additionally, there is a need to relate specific learning objectives of the literacy programs to the required abilities for entry to job-training programs. We believe that, in this environment, such action is critical to effective instruction, to retaining students in the programs, to their success in achieving the programs' objectives, and to their participating in further job-training programs. Reports on retention and success rates vary considerably, yet we found very few organizations maintaining the necessary records that form an accurate evaluation of progress.

Using Learning Styles

In the Literacy/Learning Styles Project, we have found a consistent core of cognitive characteristics in the adult population that reads at a grade 5 level which can be addressed. In the project described below, we used the Structure Of Intellect Learning Abilities Test (SOI-LA) (Meeker, 1975) to assess the cognitive abilities of clients enroled in basic literacy programs. The results showed that clients tend to work reliably in well-defined or structured environments and prefer discovery to expository approaches to tasks. They tend to be judgmental and concrete—even rigid: they do not take risks easily.

They are also easily overwhelmed with large quantities of details. Discriminating between relevant and irrelevant details is difficult. Therefore instructors must use details sparingly and clarify details regularly.

The profile found in the adults with a grade 5 reading level is very different to the cognitive pattern found in the average grade 5 learner. It is important, therefore, that strategies, environments and materials reflect the cognitive abilities that are found in the low-functioning adult population. Using elementary-grade methods and resources with adults do not match the adults' profiles and will not work. Where materials and strategies appropriate to a grade 5 learner are used, the adults see the resemblance to their earlier failures in school and simply separate themselves from further pain. This sourcebook attempts to provide you, the practitioner, with sources of appropriate information as a guide to working with some fundamental cognitive abilities of this group of adults.

The Literacy/Learning Styles Project

The purpose of the project has been to equip literacy program providers and clients with an accurate and efficient assessment of clients' learning abilities. Accurate and efficient assessments that are translatable to instruction are critical given the nature and the short duration of most programs. Teachers need to be able to understand the students' needs as they relate to the demands of the courses as quickly as possible. We believe that matching the students' learning characteristics to the stated learning objectives of the programs, instructional strategies and resources should increase the success of clients enroled in literacy programs.

Background

We assume that society requires us to possess a variety of cognitive abilities and skills. These skills form patterns or styles of thinking that characterize one's preferred way of doing things. Keefe (1979) showed that these styles decide the manner and the extent to which we interact with and process information at home, on the job, or in the community. The results of possessing and using distinctive styles and abilities show up in many ways and degrees of success in coping with life. Therefore, we cannot assume that a specific and single point on some (test) scale will separate the literate from the illiterate adult (Kirsch and Jungeblut, 1985).

The project resulted from a variety of factors:

(1) we have witnessed increasing political concern over the past decade with the "problem" of illiteracy in Canada. As a result, the popular press has promoted many articles suggesting the extent of illiteracy in Canada and projecting all possible future trends and implications of this "problem";

(2) there is little agreement among researchers and writers on a definition of "literacy" and its affiliated categories (e.g., "functional literacy"). Therefore, trends and implications often appear based on popular but unfounded assumptions and have resulted in uncertain strategies for training and employment;

(3) few literacy programs appear to have been grounded in any theory of instruction nor have they been evaluated for their effectiveness; further, dropout rates have exceeded 40% in some programs—suggesting a need to examine assessment and instruction.

Description of the Project

This three-year project evolved from a feasibility study that examined the relationship between literacy and learning (cognitive) style (Laine, 1990). We used the Structure of Intellect Learning Abilities (SOI-LA) Test (Meeker, 1975) as a way of determining (cognitive) style and applied the results to learning in classroom settings. We wanted to know if: (1) illiterate adults have a core of learning characteristics (style) that distinguishes them from other adults (cf. Marcus, 1979; Stewart, 1981), and (2) if there was any relationship between learner characteristics and instructional objectives. The study focused on adults eligible for college-based literacy programs (those with formal schooling of less than grade 8). The long-term study's primary purpose was to examine the cognitive styles of these applicants and translate them into strategies for teaching.

To gain a profile of learning abilities (styles), we asked 300 clients enroled in literacy programs to complete a special form of the Structure of Intellect Learning Abilities (SOI-LA) Test. This test is very different to the most commonly-used assessment instruments in basic skills programs, which are achievement tests. Achievement tests (cf. Laine, 1987; 1989) may reliably describe an academic difference, but their results do not explain the reasons for differences and provide no indication for specific instruction or intervention. So far, we have found the SOI-LA to discriminate in some dimensions (e.g., Systems, Memory) and to provide information that can be translated to instruction and curriculum decisions.

The Structure of Intellect Learning Abilities Test

The SOI-Learning Abilities Test is designed to examine several dimensions of Guilford's Structure of Intellect model (1967). It has both verbal and nonverbal components; it is reportedly free from contamination by school achievement; and should not be affected by variations in reading proficiency effects (Cunningham, Thompson, Alston and Wakefield, 1978; Meeker, 1969; Thompson, 1978).[1]

Guilford's model is a three-dimensional view of the intellect. Guilford defined the dimensions of the model as OPERATIONS (cognition, memory, evaluation, convergent production, divergent production), CONTENT (figural, symbolic, semantic), and PRODUCTS (units, classes, relations, systems, transformations, implications).

Within the model, the intersection of one Operation with one Content and one Product yields a specific ability, or "cell." For example, CFU (Cognition of Figural Units—visual closure), represents one ability.

When these dimensions are examined with appropriately designed tests, profiles of cognitive strengths and weaknesses can be produced that may suggest how a person processes information (Operation), which type of information the learner is most comfortable with (Content), and the type of performance the student would be most likely to achieve (Product). Meeker (1969) suggested that such profiles would not only describe, but also explain, differences among students.

---

[1] Meeker, M.N. (1969) *The structure of intellect: Its uses and applications,* Columbus, OH:Merrill.

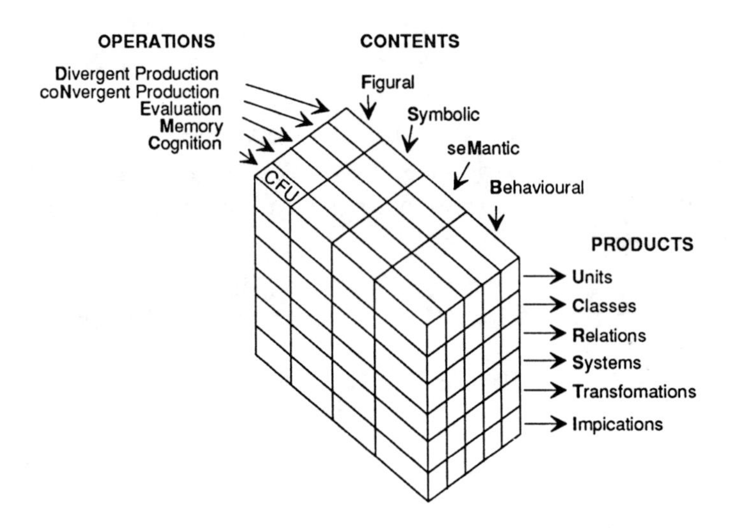

FIGURE 1: Structure of Intellect Cube

Implications for Instruction

After scoring and studying the individual and group profiles, we provided feedback—to clients and teachers—of the clients' learning styles and made recommendations for selecting instructional strategies, materials and alternative resources. Knowing the students' strengths and weaknesses encouraged teachers and students to use a greater variety of learning strategies. We have found that the Structure of Intellect model provides a profile of precursor abilities that can act as an instructional framework for teachers and can be used by students in understanding their learning environment. The knowledge gained from its use also has increased the students' autonomy.

Profile of Abilities

The following profile (Figure 2) shows the average of the scores achieved by a large group of literacy learners on the various dimensions of Guilford's model. (Note: these scores were significantly less than the average adult scores in all the dimensions.)

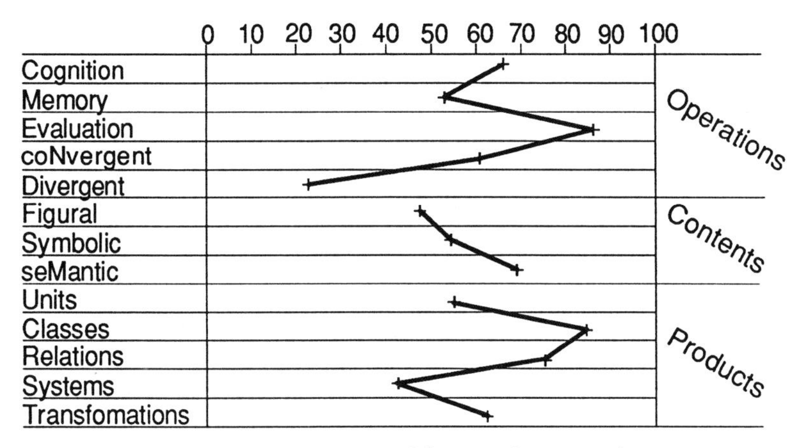

FIGURE 2: SOI Profile: Project Study

This profile is based on standard scores of the group and shows considerable variation among the dimensions. The students were relatively strong in making judgments (**E**-Operation: Evaluation), in chunking or sorting information (**C**-Product: Classes), and in discovering associations among information (**R**-Product: Relations). They work well with new material or in new situations that they can readily relate or conceptualise to something similar in their experience. They were relatively weak in recall (**M**-Operation: Memory), in seeking other solutions (**D**-Operation: Divergent Production), in knowing details (**U**-Product: Units), and in working with complex relations, sequences or routines. (**S**-Product: Systems). So, if a course or program required the students to memorize detail sequentially, then these students would be faced with information that hits their weakest abilities.

Most instructions given in learning and on-the-job do require important details to be recalled. Sequence is also critical for effective communication and successful completion of a task. (Consider forgetting how much sugar to put in a recipe and then putting it in after the flour has been folded into the mixture). In the workplace, a good eye for detail and both Memory and Systems skills are valuable and perhaps necessary abilities to have. Therefore, instructors and counsellors must appreciate that these abilities will have to be dealt with directly in class and not assume their clients can work systematically with details.

Although many consider divergent production to be a less-required ability, many people face situations where they have to deal with ambiguous tasks or unclear instructions. One has only to read the directions in a computer manual to understand the problem faced when the instructions lead one to a screen that is nothing like the description in the book. If we learn only one way to solve a problem, then any alternative is a barrier that arrests production.

Outcomes

Our studies of direct instruction in "scaffolding" (building a framework of strategies) have provided more concrete evidence of the value of recognizing learning style and translating it to instructional objectives. Currently a selection of college teachers is receiving training in the assessment and classification of their instructional materials to match learning-style dimensions. The course objectives are being prioritized by the teachers for profile matches to be made with client profiles. Ordering objectives does not mean that the content, objectives or standards have to be changed to meet or satisfy students' profiles. The object is to build instructional bridges that enable teachers to bring students toward the objectives with minimal frustration. We shall also be comparing these profiles to job-training course requirements and to career needs.

Future Directions

Future phases will build on the current training of teachers in specific instructional strategies and materials design. Participants in our intervention studies have followed through to program completion. We have re-examined their cognitive patterns in a pre-program/post-program study and have identified potential matches between their post-program profiles and entry requirements for job-training programs. These steps should: (1) expand the current instructional strategies used in literacy and preparatory programs, (2) increase the use of personalized program plans, and (3) create a bridge between literacy program goals and instructional objectives, clients abilities, and the needs of career training programs. Anyone wishing a more complete description of this study should contact: Dr. C. Laine, Faculty of Education, The University of Western Ontario, London, Ontario, Canada N6G 1G7; (519) 661–2088.

2
ADULT EDUCATION AND LITERACY

Adult Education

The practice of adult education has two proponents: those interested in grassroots literacy with social improvement in mind, and those who follow conventional institutional practices with skill acquisition as the main priority. This section is directed towards the latter but is relevant to anyone concerned with providing effective instruction in any adult learning environment. Topics within the wider area of adult education that have been considered include ethics (Brockett, 1988), student characteristics (Cross, 1981), instructional strategies (Renner, 1983), global issues that combine adult education and literacy issues (Bhola, 1989), and theory and program planning (Bundage, 1980). Selected literature of use to the relatively new practitioner include Renner, 1983; Tight, 1988; Knowles, 1980; and Cranton, 1989. The veteran practitioner will also appreciate Tough's (1971) look at change as it occurs in learning situations.

Appropriately, instructional materials are based on an interactive model of teaching and on dialogue with the learner. Boud (1987) applied this model to adults in higher learning, but the techniques are as valuable for adult basic education. The quality and quantity of discourse may be teacher-directed, but it is driven by the learner's own examination of the problem-solving process and by the learner exploring his or her perception of experience. Mezirow (1990) and Brookfield (1983) have expanded this idea with many examples.

Adults bring a wealth of prior experience to the classroom which influences their learning. Dialogue and interaction with the teacher encourages these experiences to be used and developed into learning opportunities for the student. Bright and Darville (in Taylor and Draper, 1989) examined the relationship of prior knowledge to adult learning.

With the limited time teachers have for research and development, we have included edited books (Boud and Griffin, 1987; Mezirow, 1990) to allow for reading and reflection across the field. Kidd (1973) and Tough (1971) are recognized because of the historical contribution of the authors' work and because they are still widely read and followed by adult educators. This sourcebook does not explore the politics of policy-making and funding at the administrative level, nor does it cover community-program development. These issues remain outside the scope of this project.

Readers involved in community programs and institutional settings are directed to Eric Reproduction Services, which is a repository of materials relevant to adults. Many colleges and communities can obtain abstracts of these locally.

Literacy

The sources listed reflect the ***known*** aspects of literacy; we have not included sources of "pop-literacy" and unsubstantiated opinion. Most of the articles, however, are descriptive, not empirical. There are some features that the reader should be aware of.

1. The literature is without agreement on what constitutes "literacy"—and, therefore, illiteracy. Many conclusions seem based on assumptions, surveys and "popular knowledge"; and, on context.
2. A large part of the literature is concerned with finding some point on a scale that can indicate when a person becomes literate. As a result, there are many attempts to predict which proportion of society is illiterate and the implications such predictions have for society (a focus that appears to simplify literacy to provide programs designed to "cure" the malady). A thorough discussion of these aspects can be found in *Literacy, society, and schooling* (de Castell, Luke and Egan, 1986).
3. There is no generally accepted definition, identification procedure or standard by which someone could be categorized as "illiterate."

In its most basic form, "literacy" has meant "... being able to read and write ... " (Webster's, 1984, p. 697; cf. Oxford English Dictionary, 1933). This scribal literacy is now only one of several interpretations that characterize those considered illiterate and that differentiate them from the literate part of society (Kirsch and Jungeblut, 1986). Kirsch and Jungeblut (1986) asserted that literacy may be a hierarchical complex of information-processing skills that goes beyond decoding and comprehending material.

Without any clear distinctions, "literacy" has been divided into the categories such as "functionally illiterate," "aliterate, "scribal illiterate," and "marginally literate." Each division has garnered descriptions and ranges of characteristics that further obscure the picture. The "pop" literature has also attached "literacy" to almost any adjective (we have recently seen "budgeting literacy" (National Seminars Group, 1990) such that the term appears to be translatable to "being comfortable with ... ." The reader should view the term "literacy" cautiously, since pigeon-holing our population into neat literacy categories in the absence of a consistent set of discriminating characteristics is at best a questionable activity.

Today, "literacy" has moved beyond consideration solely of reading and writing abilities to include a continuum of competencies that have a "survival value" (Kirsch and Guthrie, 1977; p. 460). This continuum implies a continuous process of applying specific skills to specific tasks (Courtenay, Stevenson and Suhart, 1982; p. 341). The term "functional competence" for example—to comprehend and to use written material—has been used to relate skills to life success: "success" being limited to education, occupation and income (American College Testing Program, 1978). There is also a problem in determining acceptable levels of success (Bormuth, 1978). Still, the studies do show that reading and writing abilities alone are not sufficient predictors of success in Preparatory or Basic Job Training programs.

If achievement scores in scribal skills alone have not provided educators with adequate indicators of a person's abilities, then there is a need to examine the notion of literacy from a different frame of reference. One such frame is Cognitive or Learning Style. This term has been variously used but is understood generally as a preferred "learning set" (Ausubel, 1968) that is a relatively stable set of strategies that influences " ... content and direction of the ongoing learning activity" (p. 314). Such patterned behaviour has been well documented (cf. Cawley, 1976; Cohen, 1969; Kagan, 1963; Laine, 1990).

Keefe (1979) showed teachers the importance of identifying specific learning (cognitive) styles in students. Accurate assessment of learning style can also help in the development of training programs for adults (Pigg, Busch and Lacy, 1980).

References

- American College Testing Program. (1978). *Adult performance level users' guide.* Iowa: A.C.T.P.

- Ausubel, D. (1968). *Educational psychology: A cognitive view.* New York: Holt, Rinehart and Winston.

- Bormuth, J. (1978). *Value and volume of literacy.* Visible language, 7, 118–161.

- de Castell, S., Luke, A. and Egan, K. (1986). *Literacy, society, and schooling.* Cambridge, England: Cambridge University Press.

- Cawley, R.W. et al. (1976). *Cognitive styles, culture conflict and non-verbal tests of intelligence.* Adult Education, 26, 101–116.

- Courtenay, Stevenson and Suhart (1982). *Functional literacy among the elderly: Where we are(n't).* Educational gerontology, 8, 339–352.

- Keefe. J. (1979). *Student learning styles: Diagnosing and prescribing programs.* Reston, VA: National Association of Secondary School Principals.

- Kirsch, R. and Guthrie, J. (1977). *The concept and measurement of functional literacy.* Reading Research Quarterly, 13, 485–507.

- Kirsch, I. and Jungeblut, A. (1986). *Literacy: Profiles of America's young adults.* Princeton, NJ: Educational Testing Service.

- Laine, C.J. (1990). A portrait of "Futures" clients and their instructional needs. In Dick, M.A. and Elrod, F. (Eds.). *Life options for exceptional individuals.* Proceedings of the fifth international conference of the Division on Career Development. Reston, VA: Council for Exceptional Children.

- National Seminar Group. (1990). *Building budgeting skills. Workshop flyer.* Scarborough, ON; Author.

- Pigg, K.E., Busch, L. and Lacy, W.B. (1980). *Learning styles in adult education: A study of county extension agents.* Adult Education, 30, 233–244.

SOURCES

2.1 Adult Education

- Apps, J. (1989). *Foundations for effective teaching.* New Directions for Continuing Education, 43, 17–27.
  Provides a framework for practitioners to examine the beliefs and values that guide adult educators. Further contends that this is the starting point for teachers who want to direct their classes through shared learning.

- Balmuth, M. (1988). *Recruitment and retention in adult basic education: What does the research say?* Journal of Reading, 31,7, 620–623.
  Based on past experiences, the article reports participant attitude toward Adult Basic Education programs. Concludes that external variables are not as important as creating an optimum learning environment for program participants.

- Barer-Stein, T. and Draper, J. (Eds.). (1988). *The craft of teaching adults.* Toronto, ON: Culture Concepts Inc.
  Articles by Thomas, Kidd and others express their commitment to a view of teaching adults that is different from teaching children. Both editors are involved in current research in the area of adult literacy.

- Bola, H.S. (1989). *World trends and issues in adult education.* London, UK: Jessica Kingsley.
  In view of the multicultural component of most groups, this volume is included to provide a historical view that could be used to form policy and plan programs. Chapter 9 focuses on methodology in adult education.

- Booth, S. and Brooks, C. (1988). *Adult learning strategies: An instructor's toolkit.* Toronto, ON: Government of Ontario, Ministry of Skills Development.
  An introduction to learning methods for adults and a compilation of successful classroom instructional models written by Ontario adult educators in colleges and community programs. It can be used as a guide to delivery techniques.

- Boud, D. and Griffin, V. (Eds.). (1987). *Appreciating adults learning: From the learners' perspective.* London, UK: Kogan Page.

  A series of articles, including submissions by Brookfield, Griffith, and Griffin intended to raise consciousness about how adults learn.

- Bright, B.P. (Ed.). (1989). *Theory and practice in the study of adult education.* London, UK: Routledge.

  An important contribution relating philosophical and psychological issues to the study of teaching in adult education. While theoretical in nature, it brings to the surface issues such as knowledge acquisition that have hereto been ignored in adult education.

- Brocket, R. (Ed.). (1988). *Ethical issues in adult education.* New York, NY: Teachers' College Press.

  One of the first books to discuss issues related to research, program planning and marketing in adult education. A must for anyone involved in the field and a good planning tool for professional development in this area.

- Brookfield, S. (1983). *Adult learners, adult education and the community.* Milton Keynes, UK: Open University Press.

  An exploration of the way in which formal educational institutions can serve informal learning for individuals and groups. A good community approach, but with instructional strategies designed to be learner-directed.

- Brookfield, S. (1986). *Understanding and facilitating adult learning.* London, UK: Jossey Bass.

  A thorough examination of ongoing theories of adult education and how they do, or do not, facilitate learning. Includes self-directed, group- and teacher-directed models of learning as challenging classroom experiences.

- Bundage, D.H. (1980). *Adult learning principles and their application to program planning.* Toronto, ON: Government of Ontario, Ministry of Education.

  Views the learner and instructor as integral and equal players in the learning process. Includes a useful bibliography relative to the field.

- Cameron, C. (1988). *Identifying learning needs: Six methods adult educators can use.* Lifelong Learning, 11, 4, 25–28.

  Discusses intuition, market analysis, surveys, self-assessment by learners, diagnostic approaches and performance analysis as possible means of assessment.

- Costa, M. (1988). *Adult literacy/illiteracy in the United States.* Santa Barbara, CA: ABC-CLIO Inc.

  An excellent handbook for research but mainly as a reference tool for planners and instructors. It is a complete guide to literacy initiatives in the United States.

- Cranton, P. (1989). *Planning instruction for adult learning.* Toronto, ON: Wall and Emerson.

  Written in handbook style for quick access to information and for comprehensibility, it includes methodology for every phase of programming, from planning to evaluation. Many models of learning are considered.

- Cross, K.P. (1981). *Adults as learners.* San Francisco, CA: Jossey-Bass.

  Considers the growing need among adults for learning opportunities. Addresses issues such as motivation, participation, and attitudes of adult students.

- Even, M.J. (1977). *A New Instructional Design Development Process for Instructors of Adults.* Nebraska, NE: University of Nebraska-Lincoln, Department of Adult and Continuing Education. (ERIC Document Reproduction Service No. ED 146 366).

  Based on recognized models in adult education such as those of Knowles, Houle and Tough, this paper combines the development, planning and evaluation of programs into a good guide for instructors given only the time, date and place of instruction (as is usually the case with community programs).

- Farmer, J., Buckmaster, A. and LaGrand, B. (1988). *Situation specific approaches.* Lifelong Learning, 12, 3, 8–13.

  Demonstrates how certain alternatives can help promote the development of this approach.

- Felmlee, D.H. (1988). *Returning to school and women's occupational attainment.* Sociology of Education, 6,1, 29–41.

  Contrasts reasons for black and white women leaving work for more schooling. It also assesses the effect of increased education on wages and job prestige for both groups.

- Jarvis, P. (1983). *Adult and continuing education, theory and practice.* New York, NY: Nichols Publishing.

  Chapters 3 and 4, in particular, focus on the psycho-social aspects of the learner, and Chapters 5 and 6 look carefully at the teaching approach (includes several models).

- Kalamas, D.J. (1987). *Prepare to work with adult learners. Module N–1 of category N—Teaching adults.* Washington, DC: Professional Education Module Series from the Department of Education.

  A teacher-education learning package for vocational educators designed to inform instructors of objective building, learning styles and adult development. Uses worksheets and self-checks with many optional activities. Good for professional development at the start of a new program when new teachers join staff.

- Kay, H. (1977). Learning and society. In M.J.A. Howe (Ed.). *Adult learning: Psychological research and application.* London, UK: John Wiley and Sons.

  Identifies issues relevant to adult literacy and adult learning with a focus on the psychological demands made on the learner and the professionals who guide instruction.

- Kidd, J.R. (1973). *How adults learn (rev.ed.).* New York, NY: Association Press.

  Kidd is to adult education as Dewey is to educational theory. The ideas will still be relevant 50 years from now.

- Knowles, M. (1980). *The modern practice of adult education: From pedagogy to andragogy (rev. ed).* Englewood Cliffs, NJ: Cambridge Adult Education, Prentice Hall Regents.

  Knowles' strength is in approaching adult education as a distinct set of theories, principles and applications. The book also includes organization and implementation strategies.

- Knox, A.B. (1986). *Helping adults learn.* San Francisco, CA: Jossey Bass.

  This volume focuses on the learning environment and the learner in it. Individual chapters such as "How to provide challenging teaching-learning interactions" can be useful in isolation.

- Lenz, E. (1982). *The art of teaching adults.* New York, NY: Holt, Rinehart and Winston.

  A short volume touching many issues relevant to adults such as "Special Learning Problems," "Teaching Special Groups," and "Teaching Roles, Styles and Techniques."

- Mezirow, J. and associates. (1990). *Fostering critical reflection in adulthood.* San Francisco, CA: Jossey-Bass.

  Anyone working with adults to help them identify their own perspectives on the world will find this valuable. Thought-provoking articles explore issues in the acquisition of knowledge.

- Ministry of Skills Development. (1988). *A directory of literacy and adult basic education programs in Ontario.* Toronto, ON: Government of Ontario, Ministry of Skills Development.

  The locations, program details (including intake procedures and a description of the types of classes) and government initiatives now in place are listed by region.

- Radcliffe, D., McDonald, C., McDougall, P. and Whyte, V. (1987). *Adults in the schools.* Toronto, ON: Government of Ontario, Ministry of Education.

  A report relevant to adults within secondary school instruction.

- Renner, P.F. (1983). *The instructor's survival kit: A handbook for teachers of adults (2nd ed).* Vancouver, BC: Training Associates.

  Applicable to many adult populations, from institutions to the workplace. Includes exercises for group-building, evaluation and communicating. Group-management techniques included.

- Rosenblum, S. and Darkenwald, G. (1983). *Effects of adult learner participation in course planning on achievement and satisfaction.* Adult Education Quarterly, 33, 3, 147–153.

  Describes a study that involved nursing supervisors in the planning phase of course design. With a control group for comparison, results showed no gains in course satisfaction. This suggests that answering the cry for "learner needs" may indicate an approach that is different from the assumed one.

- Rosenthal, N. (1990). *Active learning/empowered learning.* Adult Learning, 1, 5, 16–18.

  Contrasts passive learners and active learners, the latter identified as self-motivated, who take responsibility for their own learning.

- Smith, R.M. and Haverkamp, K.K. (1977). *Toward a theory of learning how to learn.* Adult Education, 28, 1, 3–21.

  Specifically identifies adults in learning environments with a description of learning styles and training for learning.

- Taylor, M.C. and Draper, J.A. (Eds.). (1989). *Adult literacy perspectives.* Toronto, ON; Culture Concepts Inc.

  Part 7 of this volume discusses the application of adult education principles to a number of minority groups.

- Tight, M. (1988). *Education for adults. Volume 1: Adult learning and education.* Beckenham, UK: Croom Helm.

  The chapter entitled "Processes" will facilitate teacher-student interaction models.

- Tough, A.M. (1971). *The adult's learning projects.* Toronto, ON: Ontario Institute for Studies in Education.

  Investigates the learning efforts of adults and summarizes their implications for program planning.

- Tough, A. (1982). *Intentional Change: A fresh approach to helping people change.* Chicago, IL: Follett Publishing.

  In " An Optimum Amount of Professional Control," the author looks at change as a natural part of growth in adult education. Discusses how control can improve or harm the educator's contribution in the classroom.

- Wilson, A.L. and Burket, L. (1989). *What Makes Learning Meaningful?* Paper presented at the Annual Meeting of the American Association for Adult and Continuing Education. (ERIC Document Reproduction Service No. ED 313 586)
  Reviews Dewey's, Freire's, Kolb's, and Roger's views on the role of experience in learning and argues for confronting learners with their own thinking as a means of growth and development.

2.2 Literacy

- Arnove, R. and Graff, H. (1988). *National literacy campaigns: Historical and comparative lessons.* Phi Delta Kappan, 69,3, 202–206.
  Uses a social and historical perspective to discuss what has been learned from literacy initiatives. The tension is between literacy that assigns predetermined roles for people and literacy for empowerment allowing participants a more active role in the society.

- Beder, H. and Quigley, A. (1990). *Beyond the classroom.* Adult learning 1, 5, 19–21.
  A study of non-participation in adult basic literacy programs revealing complex issues. Researchers found that these adults may or may not have aspirations that involve education.

- Bhola, H.S. (1981). *Why literacy can't wait: Issues for the 1980's.* Convergence, 14,1, 6–23.
  A theory-based discussion on literacy and the need for an aggressive policy of program distribution. Discusses the functional uses of literacy as they apply to adult illiterates.

- Bhola, H.S. (1988). *Politics of adult literacy promotion: An international perspective.* Journal of Reading, 31,7, 667–671.
  Relates to literacy training in economically depressed countries where the critical consciousness of the individual is an additional focus.

- Boraks, N. (1988). *Balancing adult literacy research and program evaluation.* Adult Literacy and Basic Education, 12,2, 66–77.

  Advocates balance in research and evaluation in seven program areas; three of these areas are problem definition versus adult competence, assumption versus honest appraisal, and reporting on controlled and uncontrolled variables.

- Brodkey, L. (1986). *Tropics of literacy.* Journal of Education, 168,2, 47–54.

  Asserts that definitions of literacy provide cultural parameters that do not always suit the learner. Dialogue with the learner can be a start in establishing a program to suit the needs of the learner, not those of the teacher.

- Cairns, J.C. (1988). *Adult literacy in Canada.* Toronto, ON: Council of Ministers of Education.

  A data-based study providing a comprehensive overview of the literacy initiative in Canada. Considers the functional role of literacy within society.

- Calamai, P. (1987). *Broken words: Why five million Canadians are illiterate.* Ottawa, ON: Southam Press.

  A journalist's view of the "dilemma." Statistics exclude natives, inmates of correctional facilities, and groups in other institutions but includes the following topics:
  - Better literacy skills crucial to the Canadian workforce;
  - Federal record on literacy: Opportunities wasted, warnings ignored;
  - Getting nowhere fast: One worker's experience;
  - Immigration boosts Canada's illiteracy rate;
  - Jury still out on what determines functional illiteracy;
  - LITERACY vs literacy: Conflict in approach;
  - National cost of illiteracy incalculable;
  - Profile of a typical illiterate;
  - What works to combat illiteracy;
  - Women more literate than men.

- Calamai, P. (1988). *Southam literacy survey.* Learning, 5,1, 6–8.

  Reports reactions to Southam Literacy Survey and probes further causes of Canadian "aliteracy." Focuses on the printed word and the acquisition of reading skills as defining a literate person. (See Willinsky, J. (1990) for rebuttal.)

- Caldwood, J. (1990). *Reading: The road to freedom.* Canadian Living Magazine, January, 39–41.
  Explores the acquisition of literacy as a struggle. The emotions involved are well described. Literacy brings relief from feelings of inadequacy and dislike for oneself.

- Carroll, J.B. (1987). *The national assessments in reading: Are we misreading the findings?* Phi Delta Kappan, 68, 424–430.
  Presents data related to reading proficiency and discusses reading proficiency in terms of literacy definitions. Suggests that proficiency starts early on in the educational process.

- de Castell, S., Luke, A. and MacLennan, D. (1981). *On defining literacy.* Canadian Journal of Education, 6,3, 7–17.
  Discusses the popular concept of functional literacy as being placed within the context of a person's life and within the behaviourist view of "high" literacy. The latter context would relate reading materials and reading capabilities to the context in which a person lives.

- Chall, J., Heron, E. and Hilferty, A. (1987). *Adult literacy: New and enduring problems.* Phi Delta Kappan, 69,3, 190–196.
  Outlines the extent of adult illiteracy and what needs to be done in terms of initiatives to alleviate it. Problems include funding, lack of trained staff and good instructional methods.

- Darville, R. (1988). *Framing il/literacy in the media.* Learning, 5,1, 9–11.
  The media here are represented by the Southam Survey and the author evaluates the value of the study in terms of what was reported and what was actually seen.

- Draper, J. (1986). *Re-thinking adult literacy.* Toronto, ON: Ontario Institute for Studies in Education, Adult Education Division.
  Identifies issues related to effective teaching practices and program and policy building. It contains references to many Canadian ABE programs.

• Erikson, F. (1988). School literacy, reasoning and civility. In Kintgen, E., Kroll, B. and Rose, M. (Eds.). *Perspectives on literacy.* Edwardsville, IL: Southern Illinois University Press.

A sociological discussion of literacy emphasizing the link between social interaction and learning. Learning tasks need to be situated in the social context of the student.

• Fingeret, A. (1988). *The politics of adult literacy education.* An address presented at the National Urban Literacy Conference, North Carolina State University. (ERIC Document Reproduction Service No. 292 053).

Considers literacy in a cultural and historical framework. Advocates looking at nonliterate adults as needing growth opportunities and empowerment if they are to become literate within the wider society.

• French, J. (1987). *Adult literacy: A source book and guide.* New York, NY: Garland.

An excellent reference book encompassing a global approach to the development of literacy. Researchers will find this very relevant.

• Fueyo, J. (1988). *Technical literacy vs. critical literacy in adult basic education.* Journal of Education, 170,1, 107–118.

Contrasts these competing views of literacy and describes one ABE program which suggests the process can be humanized.

• Gee, J.P. (1989). *What is literacy?* Journal of Education, 171,1, 18–25.

Defines literacy from the perspective of the acquisition of linguistic knowledge. This is a thought-provoking discussion which distinguishes between acquiring and learning in classroom settings.

• Graff, J.H. (1988). The legacies of literacy. In Lintgen, E., Kroll, B. and Rose, M. (Eds.). *Perspectives on literacy.* Edwardsville, IL: Southern Illinois University Press.

A theoretical discussion of literacy calling for a total approach to communicative ability rather than undue emphasis on competence determined by test scores.

- Grundin, H. (1978). *Aspects of functional literacy.* Paper presented at the Annual Meeting of the International Reading Association, World Congress on Reading. (ERIC Document Reproduction Service No. ED166 640).

  A discussion of what is regarded as a satisfactory level of literacy related to empirical studies in Sweden with an adult population. It questions whether societal demands are reasonable in terms of what is functionally necessary.

- Guthrie, J. and Mosenthal, P. (1987). *Literacy as multidimensional: Locating information and reading comprehension.* Educational Psychologist, 23, 279–297.

  Separates reading comprehension from the ability to locate information in text. Suggests the latter is a new and important step in literacy instruction.

- Guthrie, J., Schafer, W. and Hutchinson, S. (1989). *Utilities of literacy for young black and white adults.* Paper presented at the AERA Convention, San Francisco, CA., March.

  Literacy is seen as having both a cognitive and a behavioural dimension. The latter is related to time spent reading books, newspapers and other written material. This paper contends that reading achievement scores are closely related to these activities.

- Handel, R. and Goldsmith, E. (1988). *Intergenerational literacy: A community program.* Journal of Reading, 32,3, 250–256.

  Community literacy programs put the emphasis on parents' reading abilities and interaction with their children. Parents focus on their techniques and use this knowledge with their children.

- Harman, D. (1987). *Illiteracy: A national dilemma.* New York, NY: Cambridge Press.

  Takes a broad view of the problem facing the working population of mainstream America. This is a short work containing good definitions and their application to practice.

- Hayes E. and Valentine, T. (1989). *Functional literacy needs of low literate adult basic education students.* Adult Education Quarterly, 40,1, 1–14.

  Advocates that learners can do the best assessment of their literacy needs. This can be accomplished by facilitating meaningful interpersonal communication between the teacher and the learner. Encouraging disclosure of learners' problems can provide material for literacy instruction.

- Heathington, B.S. (1987). *Expanding the definition of literacy for adult remedial readers.* Journal of Reading, 31,3, 213–217.

  Review of the current definitions of literacy and suggestions for expanding them to include affective issues. For example, fear and frustration related to employment were revealed during student interviews.

- Kavale, K. and Lindsey, J. (1977). *Adult basic education: Has it worked?* Journal of Reading, 20,5, 368–375.

  Suggests that little progress has been made in achieving the promotion of adult literacy. It suggests that there is very little hard data to justify the approaches being used, that descriptions found in the literature are misleading, and that they do not relate to what is actually being done.

- Kazemek, F.E. (1984). *Adult literacy: An annotated bibliography.* Newark, DE: International Reading Association Inc.

  A compilation of general works, but does not include teaching materials or reference to specific projects. Good for the planning stage of program development.

- Kirsch, R. and Guthrie, J. (1977). *The concept and measurement of functional literacy.* Reading Research Quarterly, 13, 485–507.

  Includes the results of an adult functional reading study and occupational demands test. Proposes that practical information should form the basis for assessment to make the learner's material more relevant.

- Kirsch, I. and Jungeblut, A. (1986). *Literacy: Profiles of America's young adults.* Princeton, NJ: Educational Testing Service.

  Using the concept of the existence of a natural level of literacy skills, the author investigates the ability of

21–25-year-olds to complete specific tasks. These are related to demographics collected during interviews.

- Lazarus, R. (1982). *Reflections on creating a literate environment.* Convergence, 15,3, 67–72.
  Integrates the retention of literacy and the provision of continuing education into a policy of literacy for all.

- MacKeracher, D. (Ed.). (1984). *Women and adult basic education in Canada: An exploratory study.* Toronto, ON: Canadian Congress for Learning Opportunities for Women.
  A demographic survey which focuses on program delivery, curriculum materials and teaching in basic education programs. Another section discusses the learning and related needs of women in ABE. (See "Literacy Organizations" section.)

- Miller, G. (1988). *The challenge of universal literacy.* Science, 241,4871, 1293–1299.
  Outlines a scientific approach to determining needs for literacy and pedagogical methods required. Suggests that it may be unrealistic to think that instructional methods in reading can keep pace with technology.

- Rockhill, K. (1987). Literacy as a threat/desire: Longing to be SOMEBODY. In Gaskell, J. and McLaren, A.T. (Eds.). *Women in education.* Calgary, AB: Detselig Enterprises Limited.
  A highly charged paper exploring education as a tool for empowerment and suggesting how gender differences may dictate literacy practices. Relevant especially to practitioners with women's groups.

- Rynders, P. (1987). *The hidden problem: A guide to solving the problem of illiteracy.* Waterford, MI; Minerva Press. (ERIC Reproduction Service No. ED 290 128).
  A paper which suggests that it is becoming more and more difficult for an individual to hide the fact of his or her illiteracy.

- Sticht, T.G. (1987). *Adult literacy education.* Review of Research in Education, 15, 59–96.

  A social historical overview reviewing issues relative to a specific definition of literacy. Sees illiterate adults as being quite literate in many areas.

- Taber, S.R. (1987). *Current definitions of literacy.* Journal of Reading, 30,2, 458–460.

  Discusses definitions of literacy which are either traditional or absolute, in that they refer to years of schooling. This contrasts with definitions derived from trends in the society to which they refer.

- Taylor, M. and Draper, J. (Eds.). (1989). *Adult literacy perspectives.* Toronto, ON: Culture Concepts Inc.

  Includes many selections based on the Canadian perspective of adult education, job training, community projects and assessment tools being used in this field.

- Taylor, N., Wade, P., Jackson, P., Blum, I. and Goold, L. (1980). *Study of low-literate adults: Personal, environmental and program considerations.* Urban Review, 12,2, 69–77.

  In an attempt to develop a more concise profile of the participants in adult literacy programs, this study interviewed and documented 17 people in depth. Motivation, factors which influence progress, and coping strategies were researched, and the results were compiled.

- Thomas, A. (1987). *A decade of literacy discussion—Some reflections.* Literacy, January.

  Comments on whether the terms of discussion have changed over the last 10 years. Suggests a number of reasons that the answer is "yes" and a number that suggest the answer is "no."

- Vallentine, T. (1986). *Adult functional literacy as a goal of instruction.* Adult Education Quarterly, 36, 108–113.

  Contends that teachers who teach "functional literacy" are still involved with "Finding the Main Idea" and "Recognizing a Topic Sentence." Advocates a clear definition of the term which will allow appropriate instructional strategies, but does not indicate how that will be done.

- Willinsky, J. (1990). *The construction of a crisis: Literacy in Canada*. Canadian Journal of Education, 15,1, 1–15.
  A well-referenced, well-considered reply to the Southam survey. Advocates that educators use a broad concept of literacy within Canadian society and encourages more in-depth thinking on the issue.

3

LEARNING STYLES AND THE STRUCTURE OF INTELLECT (SOI)

Ways of Working

Do you question a ten-cent error in your till-ticket at the grocery check-out? Some people enjoy the challenge of checking the ticket. Some people feel they need to check, "just in case," and some people want to query so that these errors do not intensify. On the other hand, there are those who can't quite remember the last time they checked the till-ticket. Then, there are those who have never looked at one after the checkout person hands it over with the change; they may wonder why anyone would waste their time questioning such a small error. Of course, most people are between those extremes: they would question a $2 error—but 10 cents?

Why do people vary in the ways they approach tasks? Do we learn these behaviours from our parents? If so, then how do we explain that brothers and sisters behave differently in the same situations? Yes, people are basically different in the ways they approach situations and in what they will take time and energy over. These individual differences are not based on academic achievement, but they have tremendous implications for educators of adults, for adults have fairly consistent preferences in the ways in which they approach learning. These ways have been referred to as *styles.* To discount teaching and learning styles is to ignore the chance to make the learning environment as positive and as successful as possible.

What are (Cognitive) Learning Styles?

The sources in this section refer to a variety of ideas related to the concept of Learning Styles. A major part of learning styles is the thinking part—or a person's cognitive style. Many models of learning styles have been suggested, and a variety of instruments have been used to assess them. One such model is Guilford's Structure of Intellect. This section outlines some of these models and focuses on Guilford's model for assessment.

Specific styles of learning and thinking in adults are observed as consistent ways of responding to and processing information (Keefe, 1979; Korhonen and McCall, 1986). Numerous studies have shown constantly that students learn more, learn more easily, and remember better when taught through preferred learning styles (Dunn, 1982; Huff, Snider and Stephenson, 1986; Keefe, 1979). Among the most common models of learning styles are those based on:

1. personal experience and understanding (Hunt's Conceptual Systems Theory, 1986);
2. the impact of psychological types on interpersonal relationships and communication (Myers-Briggs Type Indicator, 1976);
3. our sets of attitudes and actions that reflect the qualities of our mental and emotional understanding of ourselves (Gregorc, 1982);
4. the ability to perceive an object separate from its context—to identify essential parts of the whole (Witkin's Field Independence-Dependence, 1976);
5. the ways in which curriculum is perceived and processed (McCarthy's 4Mat System, 1980);
6. perception and processing of information (Guilford, 1977; Meeker, 1969);
7. the effect of basic stimuli (environmental, social, emotional, physical) on one's ability to absorb and retain ideas and information (Dunn and Dunn, 1975); and
8. reliance on logical consistency and conceptual level; conceptualizing, and integrative complexity (Messick, 1976).

Any of these models may have impact for basic literacy learners. We chose to work with models related to curriculum and information processing as they are most easily translated to instruction in basic literacy classes. Also, the information processing models seemed most readily assessed through the Structure Of Intellect Learning Abilities Test (SOI-LA; Meeker, 1975).

Few studies of any of the models listed above have been able to generalize their results or have related to training programs in adult basic education (Donnarumma, Cox and Beder, 1980; Hviteldt, 1986; Pigg et al., 1980). Also, lack of a uniform idea about learning styles has hampered research in this area. However, one of the most frequently researched styles, or common group of traits, has characterized students in special programs as "field dependent" (Osipow, 1969). These students processed information tied directly to a specific situation, experience or context.

Because of the more direct association with learning information and ease of interpretation, many researchers have used the style of Field Independence/Dependence (Witkin, 1976) to identify clusters of learning characteristics. Further, Guilford (1979) showed that some cognitive style traits do influence thinking and problem solving. For example:

1. A person low on Field Independence would be less likely to see that one set of information differed from another (SOI dimension of Classes)—even if it were made up of distinct parts (p. 135).
2. Field Independence also influences educational and vocational choices that relate to the ability of seeing things from different viewpoints (SOI dimension of Transformations) (1979, p. 136).
3. Messick's Logical Consistency has been interpreted in terms of Convergent Production of Implications (Guilford, 1979, p. 136); Conceptual level and Conceptualizing has been related to the SOI dimension of Classes (Meeker, 1969), and integrative complexity to multiple Relations, or Systems (Guilford, 1979, p. 137).

Assessing Styles and Abilities

A secondary purpose of the literacy/learning styles project was to investigate the usefulness of the Meeker's Structure of Intellect (SOI-LA) Test as a measure to identify and relate traits and abilities. (A description of the Structure of Intellect model is found on pp. 18–20. For a more detailed description of the model, see Guilford (1967) *Nature of Human Intelligence*).

The full battery contains 26 tasks which cover all the dimensions of Guilford's model. The full test, however, takes over two hours to complete. Also, we found there were some subtests which frustrated the clients to the point that they gave up before engaging the task. We chose to use the subtests that were significantly related to reading (11 subtests), plus added auditory memory (2 subtests), and one divergent production subtest. We had an idea that the clients would have better auditory memory, and we wanted to see how they dealt with ambiguous tasks. So far, we have found the research form to have been reasonably reliable and to translate well to instructional objectives.

Different ability patterns of strengths and weaknesses will be observed as different approaches to learning and, therefore, will respond to different instructional strategies. It is critical, therefore, that teachers have accurate information about the client's cognitive style, so they may make appropriate instructional plans. We have found that SOI profiles provide an effective way of describing client's abilities that are readily translated to instructional plans.

Using SOI Profiles

A teacher can use the SOI dimensions to plan effective instructional approaches. The following examples demonstrate how an instructor can capitalize on the students' variety of approaches to problems. For example:

1. students can be asked what might be the "best" way of solving an everyday problem (Evaluation).
2. If more than one solution is offered, the suggestions can be collected and sorted by some criterion, e.g., amount of time involved (Classes). This offers students an opportunity to work with a problem before working on a solution.
3. The teacher can also relate the suggestions to previous work or known tasks, or make analogies (Relations).
4. At this point, the teacher could ask for other courses of action (Divergent Production) to a known problem ("What if ... ").

5. Alternatively, a teacher could approach systematic solutions by asking students to describe the steps they would take to solve the problem. Though the suggested solutions to a problem may be different, each solution would contain steps. The steps are a sequence which may be fixed or flexible. The teacher can discuss with the students the importance of some tasks having a fixed sequence of steps.
6. An activity could follow with pictures, words, or even sentences that are out-of-order. Such an activity uses the ordering (Classes) ability to uncover (Relations) a specific sequence (Systems) that solves the problem efficiently (Convergent Production).

Important Note:

The relative strength of Relations over Systems found in our samples suggests that students grasp learning new processes better through discovery than through following someone else's lead (cf. Meeker, 1969). If a course or program required the students to memorize detail sequentially, then the students in our project (see Project, pp. 14ff.) would be faced with information that hits their weakest abilities. If we learn only one way to solve a problem then our flexibility and our productivity will be greatly diminished in a rapidly changing world.

Similar situations are found where long-term workers are made redundant or are laid off. The longer and more situation-specific their employment, the more difficult it is for many adults to feel successful in retraining for alternative employment. Similarly, firms that are not able to retool or reconstruct in the face of changing markets and technology face elimination.

SOURCES

3.1 Learning Styles

- Adams, M.J. (1989). *Thinking skills curricula: Their promise and progress.* Educational Psychologist, 24,1, 25–77.

  Based on cognitive theory, the article details a program which would develop many of the skills lacking in adults and also provides an overview of other curricula already in existence. This article is only for practitioners genuinely interested in using the concept in their classroom teaching.

- Arthur, A. (1987). *Teaching and learning styles: 4Mat teaching and learning styles: A unit of study for general level business students.* Toronto, ON: Ontario Secondary School Teachers' Federation.

  Following left-mode/right-mode learning theory, the author details a content approach using different modes. Good for lesson design and for understanding how a total curriculum could be formulated around this concept.

- Cavanaugh, D.P. (1981). *Student learning styles; A diagnostic prescriptive approach to instruction.* Phi Delta Kappan, 63,3, 202–203.

  Describes the use of the Learning Style Inventory (LSI) to improve instruction. Although applicable to secondary school instruction, the instrument can also be used with adults.

- Conti, G. and Welborn, R. (1986). *Teaching/learning styles and the adult learner.* An Omnibus of Practice and Research, 9,8, 20–24.

  Using part-time students, the Canfield Learning Style Inventory, and the Principles of Adult Learning Scale for Teachers, this study found a significant relationship between teaching style and student achievement.

- Cosky, M.J. (1988). *Computer based instruction and cognitive styles: Do they make a difference?* Paper presented at the National Conference on Computer Based Education, Bloomington, MN.

  Suggests considering cognitive style in the design phase of computer implementation. The idea then follows into the development, implementation and evaluation phases.

- Dorsey, M., Oscar, L. and Pierson, M.J. (1984). *A descriptive study of adult learning styles in a non-traditional education program.* Lifelong Learning, 7,8, 8–11.

  Assesses effectiveness in guiding counsellors and faculty in dealing with adults using Kolb's Learning Style Inventory.

- Dunn, R. and Dunn, K. (1975). *Educator's self-teaching guide to individualizing instructional programs.* New York: Parker Publishing.

  Presents the Learning Style Elements model and shows how the various elements within the four basic stimuli (physical, emotional, sociological, environmental) interact to affect a learner's ability to absorb and retain information. Teachers can develop instructional strategies based on profiles from the Productivity Environmental Preference Survey.

- Dunn, R., Price, G., Dunn, K. and Saunders, W. (1979). *The relationship of learning style to self- concept.* The Clearing House, 53, 155–158.

  Appropriately discusses individualized learning and suggests that students need to know their learning style and be confident with it to work effectively with this kind of instruction. This may help learners make decisions about their options.

- Enochs, J.R., Handley, H.M. and Wollenberg, J.P. (1986). *Relating learning style, reading vocabulary, reading comprehension and computer assisted instructional modes.* Journal of Experimental Education, 54,3, 35–39.

  A study to investigate the relationship of computer-assisted instruction (CAI), traditional teaching methods and achievement. Instruction in clerical skills suggests that CAI can result in higher test scores.

- Even, M.J. (1982). *Adapting cognitive style theory in practice.* Lifelong Learning, 5, 14–17; 27.
  Relates practice to field dependence/independence learners. Includes a procedure for administrators to look at their style relative to the people they supervise. Useful for community programs where life-skills issues predominate.

- Even, M.J. (1987). *Why adults learn in different ways.* Lifelong Learning, 10,8, 22–25; 27.
  Gives background theory and strategies for reaching adults with very different ways of approaching material. Learning, while voluntary, is described as a "response to teachering." Discusses the learner's "baggage barriers" that are carried to class.

- Fagan, W.T. (1988). *Concepts of reading and writing among low-literate adults.* Reading Research and Instruction, 27,4, 47–60.
  A study investigating the reading and writing concepts held by adults reveals that they consider reading to be mainly a decoding task. Also indicates that adults see the teacher as the "giver" of literacy, thereby developing a dependency relationship which may not be good for the learner.

- Ferrell, B. (1983). *A factor analytic comparison of four learning style instruments.* Journal of Educational Psychology, 75,1, 33–39.
  Asserts that none of the instruments can address cognitive, affective and physical behaviour. Practitioners should assess the test and the student in light of this.

- Fischer, B. and Fischer, L. (1979). *Styles in teaching and learning.* Educational Leadership, 36,4, 245–251.
  Ten learning styles and six teaching styles are highlighted. While no single judgments are imposed, a style valuing conformity and dependence is not acceptable to the author.

- Florini, B. (1989). *Teaching styles and technology.* New Directions for Continuing Education, 43, 41–53.
  Recognizing one's own teaching style can facilitate the use of technological aids with students. Looks at the institutional context also.

- Gregorc, A.E. (1982). *An adult's guide to style.* Maynard, MA: Gabriel Systems.

  Overviews Gregorc's work and his ORGANON model focusing on his use of self-awareness, acceptance of other's styles, and the development of abilities to expand one's own style.

- Guild, P.B. and Garger, S. (1985). *Marching to different drummers.* Alexandria, VA: Association for Supervision and Curriculum Development.

  A thorough examination of learning styles within an educational setting. Poses relevant questions for their application to teaching.

- Hansford, S.G. (1983). *Learning never ends. A handbook for part-time teachers of adult basic education.* Jacksonville, FL: University of Northern Florida. (ERIC Document Reproduction Service No. ED 244 149.)

  Chapter 4, on teaching/learning styles, discusses incorporating psychological type and learning style in instructional planning.

- Hanson, J.R. (1988). *Learning style models: Trends, pitfalls and needed new directions.* Paper presented at the Learning Styles Conference, Toronto, Ontario (March).

  Critiques learning-style models and presents 10 good criteria by which the practitioner can evaluate them. As certain models tend to have a bandwagon following, the paper gives specific emphasis to each one.

- Huff, P., Snider, R. and Stephenson, S. (1986). *Teaching and learning styles celebrating differences.* Toronto, ON: Ontario Secondary School Teachers' Federation.

  Explores several methods of determining learning styles but uses case studies and teaching materials to apply the findings.

- Hunt, D. (1987). *Beginning with ourselves.* Cambridge, MD: Brookline.

  Using teachers' self-awareness, their knowledge of classroom interaction, and their personal experiences, Hunt suggests ways in which teachers can deal with different learning styles.

A useful down-to-earth tool for practitioners to experience renewal in a helpful way.

- Isaacs, A.F. (1987). *Creativity and learning styles.* The Creative Child and Adult Quarterly, 12,4, 249–258.
  Describes the concept of learning styles and how they function in conjunction with disabilities, teaching styles, and in different environments.

- Keefe, J. (1987). *Learning style theory and practice.* Reston, VA: National Association of Secondary School Principals.
  An overview of the individual differences in learning, in theory, research, instrumentation and practice. A final chapter on application to the classroom may be particularly helpful.

- Kiersey, D. and Bates, M. (1984). *Please understand me: Character and temperament styles (4th ed).* Del Mar, CA: Prometheus Nemesis.
  Based on the Myers-Briggs Type Indicator, this book gives a detailed account of how character types and personality styles may be compatible or in opposition in learning environments.

- Kolb, D.A. (1984). *Experiential learning.* Englewood Cliffs: NJ: Prentice Hall.
  In "Individuality in Learning and the Concept of Learning Styles," the author explores both concepts of "individuality" and "learning styles." Kolb's theory centres around descriptors such as accommodator, diverger, converger and assimilator. The method is well researched and would benefit adults who can often apply knowledge about learning style.

- McCarthy, B. (1980). *The 4MAT system: Teaching to learning styles with right/left mode techniques.* Barrington, IL: Excel Inc.
  Describes a teaching/curriculum model based on Kolb's experiential learning cycle. Includes a variety of sample lessons suitable, with some modifications, for basic education.

- Messick, S. (1976). Personality consistencies in cognition and creativity. In S. Messick (Ed.). *Individuality in learning.* San Francisco, CA: Jossey-Bass; pp. 4–33.

  A theoretical work which provides a considered foundation for understanding conceptual levels and the ways in which people conceptualize.

- Mickler, M.L. and Zippert, C.P. (1987). *Teaching strategies based on learning styles of adult students.* Community/Junior College (Quarterly of Research and Practise), 11,1, 33–37.

  Questions whether teaching styles would result in significant achievement among the students described. Uses the Productivity Environment Preference Scale for assessment. Results support previous research showing that gains in learning outcomes can be expected.

- Myers, I.B. (1962). *Introduction to type.* Palo Alto, CA: Consulting Psychologists Press.

  This is a comprehensive booklet that describes the Myers-Briggs types with reference to Carl Jung's original work on psychological types.

- O'Brien, L. (1989). *Learning styles: Making the student aware.* NASSP Bulletin, 73,519, 85–89.

  Advocates the use of learning styles to deal with diversity in the classroom. Suggests that students need to be aware of their styles and how they relate to studying and test-taking.

- Osipow, S. (1969). *Cognitive styles and educational vocational preferences and selection.* Journal of Counselling Psychology, 16,6, 534–46.

  Uses several measurements of cognitive style and the Vocational Preference Inventory; a relationship is found between functioning and vocational choice in a number of fields.

- Oxford, R. (1988). *Styles, Strategies and Aptitudes: Important Connections for Language Learners.* Unpublished working draft of a presentation for the Interagency Language Round Table.

  Currently being produced as a book, this paper describes a classroom study which links learning styles and strategies to aptitude for learning a language. It goes further in predicting language proficiency.

- Pigg, K., Busch L. and Lacy, W. (1980). *Learning styles in adult education: A study of county extension agents.* Adult Education, 30,4, 233–244.

  Using Kolb's Learning Style Inventory, the authors use the results to design effective staff training programs. Good explanation of Kolb's model included.

- Pitts, M. and Thompson, B. (1984). *Cognitive styles as mediating variables in inferential comprehension.* Reading Research Quarterly, 19,4, 426–435.

  Although the work was done with fourth, fifth and sixth grade poor and good readers, the results are relevant to older populations. Researchers suggest that comprehension may be related to cognitive style and that monitoring abilities may be style-related also.

- Robinson, K. (1985). *Visual and auditory modalities and reading recall: A review of the research.* (ERIC Document Reproduction Service No. ED272 840.)

  Highlights the relationship between visual and auditory systems and the extent to which students can recall text. Findings record the need for auditory processing.

- Rule, D. and Grippin, R. (1988). *A critical comparison of learning style instruments frequently used with adult learners.* A paper presented at the Annual Conference of the Eastern Educational Research Association, Miami Beach, Florida (25 February).

  Kolb, Myers-Briggs, Productivity Environment Preference Survey, and Self-Directed Readiness Learning Scale are examined in the light of instrument development and psychometric qualities. Creates an awareness of the fallibility of tests.

- Schaie, K.W. (1984). *Midlife influences upon intellectual functioning in old age.* International Journal of Behavioural Development, 7, 463–478.

  Looks at cognitive style and other life style variables to show what effects ability performance as the individual grows older.

- Sinatra, R. (1986). *Visual literacy connections to thinking, reading, and writing.* Springfield, IL: Charles C. Thomas.
  In "A Learning Style View of Visual Literacy," the author deals specifically with learners who prefer to think visually as a dominant mode rather than through a written mode.

- Smith, R.M. (1982). *Learning how to learn: Applied theory for adults.* Chicago, IL: Follett Publishing Company.
  Chapter 3 in this volume, entitled "Learning Styles," includes a good summary of the meaning with some applications. The remainder of the book discusses different environments for learning, all applicable to adult populations.

- Williams, L.V. (1983). *Teaching for the two-sided mind.* Englewood Cliffs, NJ: Prentice-Hall Inc.
  Includes descriptive and prescriptive information applicable to left-brain/right-brain dominance theory. While not directly applied to adults, many of the suggestions could be implemented in adult basic literacy classrooms.

- Witkin, H.A., Moore, C.A., Goodenough, D.R. and Cox, P.W. (1977). *Field-dependent and field-independent cognitive styles and their educational implications.* Review of Educational Research, 47,1, 1–64.
  Although lengthy, this article reviews a well-researched method of identifying learning styles and how it can be used in the classroom. Descriptors may be useful for practitioners.

3.2 Structure of Intellect

- Cunningham, C.H., Thompson, B., Alston, H.L. and Wakefield, J.A. (1978). *Use of S.O.I. abilities for prediction.* Gifted Child Quarterly, 22,4,506–511.
  While focusing on gifted children, this article gives several insights into how a group of teachers used the SOI for assessing children's abilities when those abilities were often hidden from day-to-day observation.

- Feldman, B. (1981). *The structure of intellect and learning to read.* University of Southern California. Unpublished doctoral dissertation.

  This work is descriptive of learning to read in children, but basic literacy teachers will gain insights into the use of the SOI to assess and focus a relationship between (learning style) abilities and reading achievement.

- Guilford, J.P. (1976). *The Nature of Human Intelligence.* New York: McGraw-Hill.

  This is the definitive work which describes the Structure of Intellect model in depth and refocuses the concept of intelligence in line with the theory. This book is a theoretical tome and not for the reader looking for classroom ideas.

- Guilford, J.P. (1977). *Way beyond the IQ.* Buffalo, NY: Creative Education Foundation.

  A brilliant practical guide for translating the Structure of Intellect model in action. Includes a translation of Structure of Intellect concepts into career education terms.

- Guilford, J.P. (1979). *Cognitive psychology with a frame of reference.* San Diego, CA: Edits Publishers.

  An introductory text in cognitive psychology which relates the Structure of Intellect to individual differences in learning. Special attention is given to the problems of learning of concepts, reinforcement and memory. There are useful sections on creative thinking, problem solving and intellectual controls which relate to learning styles.

- Guilford, J.P. (1980). *Cognitive styles: What are they?* Educational and Psychological Measurement, 40, 3, 715–735.

  A somewhat technical treatment which sees cognitive style as different dimensions in intellectual ability and relates styles to a Structure of Intellect model. Also reviews other models in the genre.

- Meeker, M.N. (1969). *The Structure of Intellect: Its interpretation and uses.* Columbus, OH: Charles E. Merrill.

  Provides the practitioner with an effective translation of Guilford's model in teaching terms. Provides good descriptions of the various components and how they may be used for curriculum planning.

NOTE: A more complete bibliography of papers related to the Structure of Intellect can be found in Guilford, J.P. *Creative Talents.* San Diego: EDITS.

4

CLASSROOM METHODS

Instructional Strategies

The following selections suggest various classroom strategies that are relevant to adult learners. These are considered tools for teachers rather than definitive techniques. The following guidelines have been adapted and compressed to assist in using the techniques outlined in the literature (United States Department of Eduction, 1990).

1. Use small portions of learning materials. Break up assignments into smaller ones.
2. Check for comprehension regularly and before proceeding into new work. This can be done by short quizzes, questioning and learner demonstrations.
3. Consider using all modes of learning (see section on learning styles). This will approach learners through their strengths.
4. Discuss "learning" with learners as an activity. Help them identify the strategies they use with the materials being presented. Describe how they can assist themselves and each other by using specific strategies. For example, if some memory work is essential, discuss how this can be done.
5. Clear instructions are a must. Look for signs of understanding and "getting it." Use multisensory approaches to assist.
6. When new written material is introduced, use semantic mapping or some other schema for introducing it. Explain this to the learner as an aid in his or her individual work.
7. Visual aids are useful. Use overheads, films, slides, flip charts, chalkboards, computer graphics and illustrations.

8. Eye contact helps learners maintain attention and encourages good listening skills.
9. Adult learners respond to dialogue. Good questioning techniques assist problem solving and self-discovery.
10. Let adults experience learning new materials and use learners' experience (prior knowledge) to build relations skills.

Some articles in the section are not only related to literacy, but also contain specific classroom strategies for enhancing the learning environment. ERIC reports are an excellent source of practitioners' materials and can be of ongoing assistance to classroom teachers.

Teacher Materials

The search for good instructional materials for adults, especially in low-level literacy classes, is by now legendary. While this shortage has not been rectified totally, some companies are awakening to the fact that adult-directed materials are badly needed.

By the same token, some of the materials used in second language learning have proved valuable because they are based on a communicative model of teaching (Steinberg, 1983; Olson, 1977).

The following pages contain a very concise sample of what is available. It is suggested that the reader investigate other materials using the list of publishers in Section 5 of this volume. They have been chosen with adults in mind.

The read-aloud suggestions similarly include possible selections. Local libraries will be the most help in this regard. There are many books explaining natural phenomena (Bowden, 1979) which can be used as the basis for discussion and for examining the adult's perception of the world. Proverbs and folk tales are also effective in drawing out an adult's prior knowledge.

Using Computers in the Classroom

The computer section has two main foci:

1. Issues in instructional design using microcomputers. What is the impact of introducing computer-assisted learning for the learner and also for the practitioner?

2. Software applications relevant to adult basic education: what will work for basic-level learners?

Instructional design, the first issue, is still in the development stage. Proponents of the use of technology for literacy instruction are at present concerning themselves with the problem of determining memory and transfer linked to computer use. This is a complex issue, with many instructional designs incorporating computers only part of the time, and classroom teaching the rest of the time. Results must be separated and identified for specific effects.

Software applications, as anyone who has tried to purchase them will know, exist in multiple variations. Teachers working in literacy programs reveal some important strategies for success with new applications. Initially, all staff must be well trained before any software is introduced into the classroom. This could be accompanied by a video presentation for adult students detailing how computers can work for them. Adult educators feel that this approach is part of the learning how-to-learn process and that it has great value for adult learners. Many teachers have used word-processing programs and are adamant that they are a useful tool in working with adults. The control given the adult learner contributes positively to their success. An additional aspect of classroom computer use should be learners teaching others in order to learn new knowledge. Often called "peer teaching" or using the learner as expert, this technique is being used successfully in many computer environments.

While general comments provide some guidelines for the use of software, ultimately, there is no alternative to testing the product personally. For specific software suggestions and evaluations from Canadian sources, see Teaching Methodology Annotated Software Evaluations and Publishers Information (Goulding, Tumpane and Watkins, 1988). However, the buyer must beware. The individuality of your clients and their specific needs and abilities must factor into the careful scrutiny of any software program for classroom use. The Adult Literacy and Technology Newsletter will help you keep in touch with new ideas. (See Journals and Newsletters.)

Occupational Literacy

While literacy initiatives in community and community college settings have stressed reading, math and life skills, initiatives in the workplace have been in two main areas. Some see workplace literacy as needing to develop the reading skills of the worker who is having to cope with more and more materials in the form of complex written instructions (Diehl and Mickulecky, 1988). This academic view of literacy results in the teaching of grammar, spelling, decoding skills and other standard forms of reading instruction. The goal is to enable the worker to handle more difficult reading tasks that will result in higher job attainment and increased potential in the job market. Others feel that workplace instruction must be tied into the functions or tasks that the worker is going to be required to do. As such, instruction must be designed and driven by the needs of these functions (Patterson, 1989).

The latter approach, which is job focused, draws on a number of specific techniques from which the curriculum may be built. These techniques were demonstrated at the Adult Literacy and Technology Conference in Minnesota (July 1990). A popular and well-designed model has the instructor tour the job site and take photographs of particular functions. Picture stories are developed, vocabulary introduced, and problem situations created. This may best be described as a communicative approach. Interactive video uses a video of a specific job function from which reading tasks are then authored.

This allows student-machine interaction on a random basis and can be used at the discretion of the employer. Still other approaches use software programs for vocabulary alone, in the hopes that literacy levels will be raised and employees will be more capable of efficient production.

Whatever the approach, literacy practitioners in workplace literacy environments express an imperative: the employer's commitment throughout. This kind of literacy instruction depends very much on the employer's needs, the effect of illiteracy on production, and the affordability of the instruction proposed. The general feeling among workplace literacy workers is that employers are undecided about placing such programs within company time. They are also unsure of the ability of these programs to affect production, failing to see the relationship between a reading test score and increased production. This is clearly an issue for future research and development and is reflected in the selections made.

SOURCES

4.1 Instructional Strategies

- Adams, M.J. (1989). *Thinking skills curricula: Their promise and progress.* Educational Psychologist, 24,1, 25–77.

  (See Learning Styles section.)

- Ayrer, J. (1977). *Problems in the development of a test for functional literacy.* Journal of Reading, 20,8, 697–705.

  Suggests that tests claiming to measure functional literacy have a hidden value system built into them. In fact, test construction is the result of a number of decisions made by the author which should be uncovered before a test is used.

- Bond, C. (1989). *Using semantic webbing to develop outlining skills.* Reading Improvement, 26,3, 194–98.

  As a schema for organizing ideas, semantic webbing can assist in vocabulary development and for increasing comprehension. The author also explains its use as an aid for student writing.

- Buder, M.N. (1988). *Oral reading and adult poor readers: Implications for practice.* Journal of Reading, 31,8, 736–739.

  Compares the negative and positive memories of poor readers who experienced read-aloud exercises during childhood. Advocates adults be given a chance to prepare materials before reading them aloud to reduce the effects of negativism.

- Cairns, J.C. (1988). *Adult literacy in Canada, a book.* Toronto, ON: Council of Ministers of Education.

  Includes a discussion of current attempts to define illiteracy and functionally literate, as well as a complete overview of all programs across Canada and how each province handles program delivery.

- Carrell, P. (1987). *Initiatives in communicative language teaching II.* Don Mills, ON: Addison-Wesley.

  Note especially a chapter entitled "Fostering Interactive Second Language Reading" which discusses bottom-up and top-down processing as it relates to reading. Schema are described for use in the teaching of reading.

- Crain, S.K. (1988). *Metacognition and the teaching of reading.* Journal of Reading, 31,7, 682–685.

  Presents the idea of a study guide which asks the student to record "What I know," "What I already knew," and "What do we need to know" as he or she reads through a passage. Would be useful for adults who can read but who are trying to improve their competence for college entry.

- Davis, Z. and McPherson, M. (1989). *Story map instruction: A road map for reading comprehension.* Reading Teacher, 43,3, 232–240.

  This model places emphasis on a pre-reading stage and offers a way of organizing the material for the student.

- Diekhoff, G. (1988). *An appraisal of adult literacy programs: Reading between the lines.* Journal of Reading, 31,7, 624–630.

  Discusses how the effectiveness of adult literacy training has been overstated and explains how this has occurred as a result of the data collected on the clients.

- Epstein, H.T. (1981). *Learning to learn: Matching instruction to cognitive levels.* Principal, 60,5, 25–30.

  Describes a teacher sensitization course. This has been developed to help practitioners assess the receptive and learning capacity of a child, but it begs experimentation in adults settings.

- Fagan, W.T. (1987). *Low readers and low comprehensible input.* Canadian Journal of Special Education, 3,1, 89–101.

  Low-reading achievers in a group of adult illiterates were studied. Results indicate that the meaning of a clause was possible, but not the meaning of whole sentences. This is consistent with practitioners' understanding generally.

- Feldhusen, F. and Treffinger, J. (1977). *Teaching creative thinking and problem-solving.* Dubuque, IO: Kendall/Hunt.

  Two chapters, "Methods of Teaching Creativity and Problem Solving" and "How to Get a Project Started in Your Classroom," serve as guidelines for discussion related to the title. Examples provided can be used in the lowest-level literacy groups and tied into writing activities.

- Fiore, K. and Elasser, N. (1988). Strangers no more—A liberatory literacy curriculum. In Kintgen, E., Kroll, B. and Rose, M. (Eds.). *Perspectives on literacy.* Carbondale and Edwardsville, IL: Southern Illinois Press.

  Particularly valuable for single-gender literacy groups where critical theories of instruction may be important. This is a case history of one teacher's approach focusing on the learner's environment in the development of reading and writing materials.

- Gickling, E.E. (1990). *The integrated reading assessment strategy: A CBA alternative to traditional reading assessment.* Paper presented at the 68th Annual Convention of the Council for Exceptional Children, Toronto, Canada (April).

  Reading performance is assessed using a graded passage and oral reading with the student. This is a step-by-step procedure, and the author presents questions to consider in each phase. The process can be used to help select reading material.

- Goodman, K.S. (1985). *On being literate in an age of information.* Journal of Reading, 28,5, 388–392.

  Identifies the components of a successful literacy program. Contends that literacy level is relative to the ability to use written language and the degree to which that is necessary for specific purposes in life.

- Gordon, C.J. (1985). *Modeling inference awareness across the curriculum.* Journal of Reading, 28,5, 445–447.

  Teachers model a think-aloud process for the classroom which can be used to explore meaning in text. (See Schewell and Waddell for a full description of these strategies.)

- Griffith, M., Jacobs, B., Wilson, S. and Dashiell, M. (1988). *Changing the model: Working with unprepared students.* Community/Junior College Quarterly, 12,4, 287–303.
  Outlines Project Bridge for non-traditional minority college students who lack basic skills for courses. Program goals and curricular strategies are included.

- Guthrie, J.T. (1980). *Classrooms and battalions.* Journal of Reading, 24,4, 364–366.
  Concern for understanding basic skills in a functional context compared to school learning prompted this letter.

- Guthrie, S., Schafer, W. and Hutchinson, S. (1989). *Utilities of Literacy of Young Black and White Adults.* Presented at the AERA Convention, San Francisco, CA (April).
  Statistical analysis of literacy as it relates to occupational status and achieving a place in the larger society. Useful for urban centres where attention to cultural issues would be useful in instruction.

- Handel, R. and Goldsmith, E. (1988). *Intergenerational literacy: A community college program.* Journal of Reading, 32,3, 250–256.
  Improving the literacy status of students who are parents by using their children and "bridging" literature.

- Heaton, J.B. (1990). *Classroom testing.* New York, NY: Longman.
  Many adaptable ideas for writing, listening, speaking, reading, and writing tests. A very good treatment of the subject.

- Henneberg, S. (1986). *What do you mean, you can't read?* English Journal, 75,1, 53–55.
  Describes the need for adult materials. The author also advocates low adult/teacher ratio and recommends that adult literacy instructors should be taught the special skills required for teaching basic adults.

- Howard, J. (1988). *Adult literacy in West Germany: The paradox of success.* Journal of Reading, 31,3, 257–260.
  An overview of literacy issues reflecting the three groups into which adult illiterates fall: (1) knows the alphabet and can

write name, (2) reads short paragraphs but makes many writing errors, and (3) reads well, but doesn't write. Other observations provide implications for Canadian practices.

- Hunkins, F.P. (1985). *Helping students ask their own questions.* Social Education, 49,4, 293–295.
  Suggests that adults are adept at evaluation. The techniques in this article use that skill to develop questions that will help them think about information.

- Ingram, C. and Dettenmaier, L. (1987). *LD college students and reading problems.* Academic Therapy, 22,5, 513–518.
  Although their intellectual capability was high, university students tested as having high performance and low verbal ability generally had reading scores as low as grade 10, although math functioning was normal. Failure to use specific reading strategies was evident.

- Irvin, J. (1990). *Reading and the middle school student.* Needham Heights, MA: Allyn and Bacon.
  All the techniques outlined in this volume are applicable to adults. It also contains well-documented descriptions of other classroom strategies to improve reading skills. See especially "Building Background Information and Activating Prior Knowledge."

- Johnson, L. (Ed.). (1980). *Reading and the adult learner.* Newark, DE: International Reading Association.
  Advises that the concept of remediation be used in a positive way to develop adult skills. Considers all levels in classroom settings.

- Jones, E. (1981). *Reading instruction for the adult illiterate.* Chicago, IL: American Library Association.
  Presents strategies based on knowledge of adults as learners and of learn-to-read processes.

- Kaminsky, S., Hrach, E. and Harrison, R. (1988). *Positive reinforcement and self-evaluation accuracy influence on reading and writing.* Adult Literacy and Basic Education, 12,1, 33–43.

  An investigation of college students to see what the relationship might be between prior reinforcement and self-evaluation accuracy. Learners were more accurate in judging their own writing performance than they were when teachers had provided prior reinforcement for correctly written materials. This indicates that learners need explicit instructions in carrying out self-evaluation tasks.

- Kavale, K. and Lindsey, J. (1977). *Adult basic education: Has it worked?* Journal of Reading, 20,5, 368–376.

  Although dated, in some respects, the article is still timely in addressing the issues relevant to successful ABE program delivery. The call for hard data to validate adult teaching strategies is pertinent and still remains unanswered today.

- Kazemek, F. (1988). *Necessary changes: Professional involvement in adult literacy programs.* Harvard Educational Review, 58,4, 464–487.

  Discusses political and institutional factors in effective literacy instruction and offers holistic methodology based on dialogic and socially-oriented instructional strategies.

- Kazemek, F. (1988). *Women and adult literacy: Considering the other half of the house.* Lifelong Learning, 11,4, 23–24, 15.

  Looks at the central characteristic of "women's ways of knowing." There are some immediate implications for adult literacy instruction and some possible directions for future research.

- Keefe, D. and Meyer, V. (1988). *Profiles of instructional strategies for adult disabled readers.* Journal of Reading, 31,7, 614–619.

  Contains strategies for beginning adult readers and the next level up. This includes talking about the strategies that good readers use.

- Lipson, M.Y. and Wickizer, E.A. (1989). *Promoting self-control and active reading through dialogues.* Teaching Exceptional Children, 21,2, 28–32.
  Adults have skills which can be used to increase meaning. The author identifies how teacher-student talk can work toward this end.

- Love, L. (1985). *Learning together: A handbook for teaching adults with learning materials.* Nanaimo, BC: Malaspina College. (ERIC Document Reproduction Service No. ED 263 328.)
  Addresses post-secondary instructors of learning disabled students. Documents four case histories and discusses class strategies and identification of problems relative to classroom work.

- Mercier, L.Y. (Ed.). (1981). *Outlook for the 80s: Adult literacy.* US Department of Education, Basic Skills Improvement Program. (ERIC Document Reproduction Services No. ED. 211 701.)
  Four papers including "Modern Adult Basic Education: An Overview," "Critical Issues in Adult Literacy," "Adult Basic Education Instructional Strategies: Their Design and Improvement," and "The Care and Feeding of Instructors of Adult Literacy and Basic Education." The second paper discusses recruitment and retaining participants in programs. Attempts to define literacy and relative teaching approaches that would be effective.

- Meyer, V. (1987). *Lingering feelings of failure: An adult student who didn't learn to read.* Journal of Reading, 31,3, 218–221.
  A case history of an adult with an unstable family background who was expelled from his senior high school year for behavioural reasons. The author recounts the story, including the methodology used to help him learn to read, then and now.

- Meyer, V. and Keefe, D. (1988). *The Laubach way to reading.* Lifelong Learning: An Omnibus of Reading and Research, 12,1, 8–10.
  Examines the sounding-out approach used in the series and the weaknesses inherent in it. Evidence includes current research on interactive processes.

- Moore, B. (1988). *Achievement in basic math skills for low performing students: A study of teachers' effect and computer-assisted instruction.* Journal of Experimental Education, 57,1, 38–44.
  A study indicating that teaching methodology is more important than what we teach. Teacher attitudes, expectations and interpersonal interactions may be just as important as the curriculum.

- Mudd, N. (1987). *Strategies used in the early stages of learning to read: A comparison of children and adults.* Educational Research, 29,2, 83–94.
  A good statistical study suggesting that, although mature in years and experience, adults are not aware of different strategies for reading, and they need to be taught. Content is important for beginning adult readers and should be evaluated carefully.

- National Assessment of Educational Progress. (1987). *Students aren't literate enough.* American School Board Journal, 174,6, 14.
  Explains that the requirements of being considered literate are rising, and so are the number of people unable to meet those requirements.

- Nessel, D. and Jones, M. (1981). *The language experience approach to reading.* New York, NY: Teachers College Press.
  This technique has been used successfully by volunteer tutors and in remedial classes for many years. It is a complete description of the process and includes an evaluation component.

- Norman, C. and Malicky, G. (1986). *Literacy as a social phenomenon: Implications for instruction.* Omnibus of Practice and Research, 9,7, 12–15.

  Suggests that immersion in second language learning and adult literacy instruction are comparable. Practitioners need to recognize that self-worth and independence are a key requirement.

- Norman, C., Malicky, G. and Fagan, W.T. (1988). *Reading process of adults in literacy programs.* Adult Literacy and Basic Education, 12,1, 14–25.

  A study advocating reading as an interactive process wherein the teacher-learner relationship becomes collaborative.

- O' Malley, J.M. et al. (1985). *Learning strategy applications with students of English as a second language.* Teachers of English as a Second Language Quarterly, 19,3, 557–584.

  Not just for second language teachers, this study indicates that the strategies outlined can facilitate learning. Includes a comprehensive list of learning strategy definitions and a student interview guide to determine the best one to teach.

- Padak, G. (1987). *Guidelines and a holistic method for adult basic reading programs.* Journal of Reading, 30,6, 490–496.

  Outlines theory-based instruction which focuses on the needs of the learner.

- Padak N. and Padak, G. (1988). *Writing instruction for adults, present practices and future directions.* Lifelong Learning: An Omnibus of Practice and Research, 12,3, 4–7.

  This study about writing instruction in adult basic education courses encourages writing as an integral component for "learning, knowing and composing the mind."

- Patterson, P. (1979). *How to operate an individualized learning centre. A handbook for teachers of adult basic education.* Columbus, OH: Ohio State Department of Education. (ERIC Document Reproduction Service No. ED 220 606.)

  This guide is a beginning-to-end analysis of the process for beginning or experienced ABE teachers. It includes descriptive literature on learner characteristics.

- Perin, D. (1988). *Schema activation, cooperation and adult literacy instruction.* Journal of Reading, 32,2, 54–62.

  The author activated students' background knowledge before presenting reading material. Used a cooperative task in which reading activity was embedded. Presents steps for cooperative schema activation, reading and discussion.

- Powell, W.R. (1977). *Levels of literacy.* Journal of Reading, 20,6, 488–492.

  Attempts to categorize literacy into levels related to the function of the skills necessary in a societal context.

- Ross, J.M. (1988). *Learning and coping strategies of learning disabled students.* Adult Literacy and Basic Education, 12,2, 78–90.

  Relates coping strategies used in reading, spelling, and life skills.

- Sanders, D. and Sanders, J. (1983). *Teaching creativity through metaphors.* New York, NY: Longman.

  In "The Experiential Learning Model," a step-by-step process is presented which integrates the use of metaphors as a teaching tool. Although a relatively new concept, the practical aspect of this idea makes it worth investigating. Many learners are unaware of their use of metaphors.

- Scales, A.M. (1984). *Thinking-based strategies to enhance reading for adult learners.* Pittsburg, PA: University of Pittsburg. (ERIC Document Reproduction Service No. ED 274 945.)

  Discusses adult learners as they approach reading tasks and the strategies that they use. Uses discovery and the receptive approach to look at learning in adults. Six implications are highlighted.

- Schewel, R.H. and Waddell, J.G. (1986). *Metacognitive skills: Practical strategies.* Academic Therapy, 22,1, 19–25.

  Detailed are self-questioning, lookback strategies, using a code and inference modelling—four techniques that teachers can teach to encourage learners to take a more active role in reading.

- Schneider, S. and Cook, J. (1989). *A longitudinal analysis of adult literacy students in New York city: A two-year study.* New York, NY: Metis Associates.

  A final report which includes a database containing ethnographic information on students, hours of instruction, test results, and other selected data.

- Shuman, R.B. (1989). *Some assumptions about adult reading instruction.* Journal of Reading, 32,4, 349–355.

  Notes that literacy in adults takes longer than the six months we usually allow for the process. The article is a good overview of the pitfalls of literacy instruction.

- Silvernail, D. (1986). *Teaching styles as related to student achievement.* Washington, DC: National Education Association.

  An excellent booklet for a teacher resource centre. It tries to encapsulate teaching activities that will enhance student learning. Well organized and easily adapted to adult settings.

- Steinley, G. (1989). *Comprehending and using text ideas: The order of processing as affected by reader background and style.* Reading Horizons, 29,3, 205–214.

  A research study examining how prior knowledge and the reader's style of processing affect thinking.

- Strong, R.W., Silver, H.F. and Hanson, R. (1988). *Integrating teaching strategies and thinking styles with the elements of effective instruction.* Educational Leadership, 42,8, 9–15.

  Discusses how various strategies can be used to teach the curriculum in such a way that student thinking is developed and enhanced.

- Taylor, N., Wade, P., Jackson, P., Blum, I. and Goold, L. (1980). *A study of low-literate adults: Personal, environmental, and program considerations.* The Urban Review, 12,2, 69–77.

  Ethnographic study of participants 16–35 in six literacy programs. Evidence collated to describe such characteristics as reading habits, motivation to learn, and others in an effort to relate these to instruction.

- United States Department of Education. (1990). *Instructional strategies for adults with learning disabilities.* Washington, DC: Clearinghouse on Adult Education and Literacy, United States Department of Education; Division of Adult Education and Literacy.

  A succinct list of strategies which can be kept on hand in the classroom. A summary of a few of the strategies is found in the introduction to this section.

- Wade, S.E. (1989). *Using think-alouds to assess comprehension.* The Reading Teacher, 43,7, 442–451.

  The author has developed an informal assessment tool that will indicate how readers obtain meaning from text. The procedure is well-outlined, and examples of dialogue with each type of reader are included.

- Weinstein, C.G. and Alexander, P. (1988). *Learning and study strategies.* Toronto, ON: Academic Press.

  See especially "Approaches to Instruction in Learning and Study Strategies" (part III). This section contains selections by a number of people dealing with individual differences, English as a second language applications, and reading comprehension strategies. Good for teacher reference section of any library.

- Winser, W. (1988). *Readers getting control of reading.* Australian Journal of Reading, 11,4, 257–268.

  A self-report analysis detailing strategies readers use during and after reading text. It is highly recommended that teachers raise learners' awareness of the nature and effectiveness of reading strategies.

4.2 Teacher Materials

- Adams, J. (1974). *Conceptual blockblusting.* San Francisco, CA: W.H. Freeman.

  A wide range of exercises designed to develop a divergent attitude to problem solving, discussing blocks to successful thinking. Good for demonstrating learning strategies.

- Banman, H. and Whitehead, R. (1967). *Riddler.* New York, NY: Addison-Wesley.

  An excellent read-aloud book for adults (288-word total) about two men with a modified '51 Cadillac.

- Billings, H. and Stone, M. (1990). *1. Great Disasters. 2. Great Escapes. 3. Great Mysteries. 4. Great Rescues.* Vancouver, BC: Steck-Vaughan.

  Suitable for beginning readers, these stories can be used with semantic mapping techniques emphasizing prior knowledge. (See also Bond, C. (1989) in Classroom Methodology section.)

- Darrow, H.F. (1986). *Independent activities for creative learning (2nd ed).* New York, NY: Teachers College Press.

  Addresses learner abilities from disabled to gifted, with independence as a focus and creativity as a goal. Hundreds of good ideas presented.

- English, F.W. and Kaufman, R. (1975). *Needs assessment: A focus for curriculum development.* Washington, DC: Association for Supervision and Curriculum Development.

  In the chapter "How the Curriculum Developer does a Needs Assessment," a model using outcomes as a central concept details a step-by-step process which can be followed by any program coordinator. It is included here for teachers because it can be useful for identifying areas of concern.

- Gairns, R. and Redman, S. (1986). *Working with words: A guide to teaching and learning vocabulary.* New York, NY: Cambridge.

  Not just vocabulary exercises, this book includes games designed to teach vocabulary within a context. Included are good examples of classification and mapping exercises.

- Hendrickson, J. and Labarca, A. (1979). *The spice of life.* New York, NY: Harcourt Brace Jovanovich.

  About half the stories could be mapped semantically with learners who have just learned to read. Others could be used as a discussion base. All are high-interest passages. Good for ESL mix.

- Hoerchler, S., Hollis, J. and Richardson, D. (1990). *Language quicktionary.* East Moline, IL: Lingui Systems.
  Employs vocabulary and semantics in a word-learning game. Cards are provided with six clues to a mystery word. There are no animations on the card and the concept is good for adults.

- Huizenga, J. (1990). *Looking at American Signs.* Lincolnwood, IL: National Textbook.
  Contains a good selection of real-life pictures with questions about each one. Canadian content would be very similar. Good for evaluation skills and inference at all levels of reading. Others in the series cover food, recreation and holidays, but should be viewed for content bias.

- Krulik, S. and Rudnick, J.A. (1987). *Problem-Solving.* Boston, MA: Allyn and Bacon.
  A book of activities and non-routine problems to give students experience in problem solving. Can be used with very basic-level readers orally and in small groups with the next level up. Pick and choose to suit your purposes, because not all of them are appropriate.

- Kuchinskas, G. and Radeneich, C. (1986). *The Semantic Mapper.* Gainsville, FL: Teacher Support Software.
  This is a customized program for use with the apple computer and based on a prior knowledge framework. Included are specific activities to expand experience with computers.

- Ladousse, G.P. (1983). *Speaking personally: Quizzes and questionnaires for fluency practice.* New York, NY: Cambridge University Press.
  Uses everyday language with a selection of exercises to improve social communication. Provides a thematic structure chart for assistance with curriculum planning.

- Lazzari, A. and Peters, P. (1987). *Help 1 and Help 2 handbook of exercises for language processing.* East Moline, IL: Lingui Systems.
  These volumes grant limited reproduction rights to teachers. They contain exercises to build classification skills and

understanding of common words, but should be teacher-directed. Perfect for beginning readers and one level up where categorization, discrimination and memory need development.

- Maley, A., Duff, A. and Grellet, F. (1980). *The mind's eye, using pictures creatively in language learning.* New York, NY: Cambridge University Press.
  Pictures combine with specific exercises to develop descriptive language in a creative way. Can be used individually or with a group.

- McCormick, D., Naget, R. and Zecevic, N. (1984). *The basic bridge.* Toronto, ON: Secondary School Teachers' Federation.
  An excellent resource book profiling learners with specific problems. Includes content-related activities applicable to literacy groups. Highly recommended.

- Meeker, M. (1979). *SOI sourcebooks.* Vida, OR: SOI Systems.
  A series of books at the basic and advanced aptitude level with exercises designed to develop cognitive skills necessary for learning. Contents relate to specific dimensions on the Structure of Intellect Test. (See Introduction for more information on the model.)

- O'Connor, M. and Vorce, P. (1990). *Cognitive connections.* East Moline, IL: Lingui Systems.
  Presents visual stimuli to encourage verbal and non-verbal responses to everyday problems. Predicting, determining cause, and formulating solutions are practised.

- Olson, J.E. (1977). *Communication starters and other activities for the ESL classroom.* Hayward, CA: Alemany Press.
  Includes a number of activities that could be used in adult basic literacy with possibilities for writing activities to follow. Excellent for small group work.

- Rinvolucri, M. (1984). *Grammar games: Cognitive affective and drama activities for EFL students.* New York, NY: Cambridge Press.

  Many ideas for literacy students too. Class members can work together to put the games together and can design their own after seeing one example. Pick and choose as usual.

- Ross, E.P. (1989). *How to use the whole language approach.* Adult Learning, 1,2, 23–4, 27, 29.

  A good guide for implementing this method. It makes use of prior experience as a teaching strategy.

- Steinberg, J. (1983). *Games language people play.* Scarborough, ON: Dominie.

  Explains 88 games to be used for language arts to build a number of reading readiness skills, with some more advanced. Little preparation is needed to implement them, and adults seem to enjoy this context for learning.

- Underwood, J. (1989). *Teaching listening.* New York, NY: Longman.

  Listening is included in the sense of listening and understanding. Exercises are included with a thorough explanation of listening as an integral component of language learning.

- ————(1985). *Thumbs up.* Kilbride, ON: Kilbride Educational Services.

  A problem-solving game designed to develop divergence by presenting situations where multiple solutions are possible.

- ————(1986). *Cinematix.* London, ON: Rumours Games.

  A game to develop memory and understanding of selected groups of words at different levels. Can be used orally or through reading.

- ————(1989). *Pictures for language learning.* Cambridge, UK: Cambridge Handbooks for Language Teachers.

  Want to teach verb tense visually? Need some good ideas to integrate visual aids with writing? You can teach semantics most effectively with pictures. These and hundreds of other ideas are included for basic to advanced level. Belongs on every reference shelf.

Read-Aloud Suggestions

- Allsburg, C.V. (1985). *The polar express*. Boston, MA: Houghton Mifflin.

  An adult reflects on a magical train ride on Christmas Eve that takes him to the North Pole. The language is mature enough to make this interesting for adults.

- Bell, W. (1988). *The cripples club*. Toronto, ON: McClelland and Stewart.

  The main character has suffered memory loss as a result of his escape from war-torn Asia. The story is one of survival through the help of classmates with various disabilities who become constant friends.

- Bernstein, M. and Kobrin, J. (1974). *How the sun made a promise and kept it*. New York, NY: Charles Scribner.

  A Canadian Indian myth relating the story of a man who wants to catch the sun to make the earth warmer. Good for adults.

- Bowden, J.C. (1979). *Why the tides ebb and flow*. Boston, MA: Houghton Mifflin.

  A folktale to explain why the tides rise and fall. Good for divergent thinking to explain other phenomena.

- Devlin, H. (1975). *Tales of Thunder and Lightening*. New York: Parents Magazine Press.

  Presents a dozen different folk tales to explain lightening and thunder. Good for evaluative skills and looking at alternatives.

- Gzowski, P. (1987). *The new morningside papers*. Toronto, ON: McClelland and Stewart.

  Short and simple, these stories reflect Canadian life perfectly for read-aloud purposes. May be followed up with story-writing or recording activities.

- Mowat, F. (1956). *Lost in the Barrens.* Toronto, ON: McClelland and Stewart.

  About the Far north, a Cree Indian boy and his Canadian friend who have a wilderness adventure that tests their skills for dealing with the environment. Survival is the theme and adults can relate to the trials and tribulations.

- Peterson, G. (1968). *Proverbs to live by.* Kansas City, KS: Hallmark Cards.

  Read them, discuss them, display them, or hand them around, but use them. Much of the language used is at a low level and they are short enough for ESL students. Good warm-up exercises.

- Procunier, E. (1982). *Searchlights: Selected essays.* Toronto, ON: Book Society of Canada.

  Only for read-aloud, it contains well-known Canadian and American authors with stories of timeless appeal.

- Smucker, B. (1977). *Underground to Canada.* Markham, ON: Penguin.

  A fast-moving story that recounts an escape from Mississippi to Canada. Based on the narrative experiences of fugitive slaves and other actual events. The author has avoided dialect in recounting the tale and has told it in plain language.

- Wilson, E. (1982). *Disneyland hostage.* Toronto, ON: Clarke Irwin.

  An exciting mystery occurs when terrorists strike Disneyland and grab one of the visitors. See also by the same author: *Murder on the Canadian, Vancouver Nightmare, Terror in Winnipeg, The Lost Treasure of Casa Loma*, and *The Ghost of Lunenberg Manor.*

4.3 Using Computers

- Beattie, E. and Preston, N.R. (1989). *Selecting microcomputer software.* ERIC Digest. Syracuse, NY: ERIC Clearinghouse on Information Resources.

  Provides basic steps in courseware evaluation and selection with specific criteria included for each step.

- Bernardon, N.L. (1989). *Let's erase illiteracy from the workplace.* Personnel, 66,1, 29–32.

  Examines the use of interactive video programs to help employees use basic skills. Although expensive, the technique allows the employee to work on vocabulary and reading tasks related to a specific job sight.

- Collins, B. (1987). Adolescent females and computers: Real and perceived barriers. In Gaskell, J. and McLaren, A.T. (Eds.). *Women in education.* Calgary, AB: Detselig Enterprises Limited.

  Describes both qualitative and quantitative differences between male and female access to computer opportunities. Provides a framework of the barriers with intervention strategies.

- Cosky, M.J. (1988). *Computer-based instruction and cognitive styles: Do they make a difference?* Paper presented at the National Conference on Computer Based Education, Bloomington, MN.

  (See "Learning Styles" section.)

- DeGroff, L. (1989) *Is there a place for computers in whole language classrooms?* Journal of Reading, 43,8, 568–572.

  The issues discussed here are pertinent to adults even though the article is about children's learning. Social interaction, time and choice of use, real purposes and audiences, process approaches, and risk taking can all be transferred into practices for adults.

- Dick, W. (1987). *Instructional design and the curriculum development process.* Educational Leadership, 44,4, 54–56.

  Details a systems approach, giving an eight-step process. Includes a feedback loop for evaluation and revising. Good for the instruction planning stage and includes behaviourally stated instructional goals.

- Enochs, J.R., Handley, H.M. and Wollenberg, J.P. (1986). *Relating learning style, reading vocabulary, reading comprehension and computer-assisted instructional modes.* Journal of Experiment Education, 54,3, 35–39.

  (See "Learning Styles" section.)

- Florini, B. (1989). *Teaching styles and technology*. New Direction for Continuing Education, 43, 41–53.
  (See "Learning Styles" section.)

- Giganti, P. (1989). *Creating student handouts with a Macintosh computer*. Computing Teacher, 24–28.
  Using either MacDraw, MacDraft, Superpaint or Works 2.0, detailed instructions are provided for producing understandable handouts.

- Hedley, C.N. (1986). *Software feature: What's new in software? Computer programs for the adult learner*. Journal of Reading, Writing and Learning Disabilities International, 2,4, 349–363.
  Reviews adult-learning principles and lists software suitable for reading, writing, career development and word processing.

- Hopwood, T. (1989). *The use of the word processor in the teaching of English as a foreign language to adults*. Cambridge, MA: Bell Educational Trust. (ERIC Document Reproduction Service No. 312 892.)
  Both a discussion of the use of word processors and also a report of a survey of teacher attitudes. The latter may help avoid some of the pitfalls. Teacher education seems to be a major contributor toward the success in the integration of computers.

- Kuchinskas, G. and Radeneich, M. (1986). *The Semantic Mapper*. Gainsville, FL: Teacher Support Software.
  (See "Teacher Materials" section.)

- Lieberman, J. (1987). *Implications of adult learning characteristics and learning style for the design of software documentation*. Technical Writing Teacher, 14,2, 219–231.
  Uses adult learning principles and findings to conclude that software documentation should consider the user's prior knowledge.

- McClintock, R.O. (Ed.). (1988). *Computing and education: The second frontier.* New York, NY: Teachers College Press.
  A series of articles exploring computers as intelligent tools that need to be controlled and directed for effective use. Good for programs and curriculum planners.

- Mills, H. and Dejoy, K. (1988). *Applications of educational technology in a self-directed learning program for adults.* Lifelong Learning: An Omnibus of Practice and Research, 12,3, 22–24.
  Explains computer-assisted learning in terms of learner control. Although applicable to higher-level students, many of the ideas can be applied to literacy programs that are currently self-directed.

- Moore, B. (1988). *Achievement in basic math skills for low performing students: A study of teachers' affect and computer-assisted instruction.* Journal of Experimental Education, 57,1, 38–44.
  (See "Classroom Methodology" section.)

- Nurss, J.R. (1989). *PALS Evaluation Project.* Atlanta, GA: Georgia State University. (ERIC Document Reproduction Service No. ED 313 573.)
  PALS is an IBM curriculum which integrates the use of interactive video and word processing into a language arts program. This controlled study suggests that adults, whether in a computerized or traditional classroom, performed equally well. Gains were noticed in typing skills. The bottom line is still "use with caution."

- Rayman, J.R. (1981). *Computer-assisted career guidance for adults.* New Directions for Continuing Education, 10, 77–83.
  Includes an overview of career development theory as it applies to adult learners. The main portion of the article describes DISCOVER, a system of career search and exploration for adults.

- Reinking, D. (1989). *Misconceptions about reading and software development.* The Computer Teacher, 16,4, 27–29.

  Details such misconceptions as "reading is best taught by focusing on specific skills in isolation" and "reading comprehension is a product, not process."

- Reissman, R. (1990). *Compucare centre: An activity for the one-computer classroom.* Computing Teaching, 18,1, 8–9.

  A very imaginative idea uses the computer as a problem solver. Students input class or personal problems, others help solve them. A compucare coordinator provides student management. Good for enhancing self-esteem and collaborative learning.

- Rizza, P.J. and Walker-Hunter, P. (1979). *New technology solves an old problem: Functional literacy.* Audiovisual Instruction, 24,1, 22–23, 63.

  Evaluation of the Basic Skills Learning System, which uses a computer-based instructional system with curricula in basic reading, language and math.

- Rude, R. (1986). *Teaching reading using microcomputers.* Englewood Cliffs, NJ: Prentice-Hall, Inc.

  A general descriptive book for software and for a closer look at classroom methodology. Not particularly graded.

- Seaman, D. (1988). *An evaluation of computer-assisted instructional systems used to deliver literacy services for JTPA participants at Houston Community College.* Houston, TX: Texas Center for Adult Literacy and Learning. (ERIC Document Reproduction Service No. ED 311 226.)

  Reports on the use of computers to teach basic skills and advocates computer-assisted instruction as most effective when integrated with teacher/student instruction.

- Turner, T. (1988). *An overview of computers in adult literacy programs.* Lifelong Learning, 11,8, 9–12.

  PLATO, PALS and CCC (Computer Curriculum Corporation) are discussed as to curriculum content, instructional hours, philosophy, features and other characteristics. Presents purchasing guidelines for other technology.

- Vockul, E. (1990). *Instructional principles behind computer use.* Computing Teaching, 18,1, 10–15.
  Provides some background reading on the implementation of instructional techniques for teachers relatively new to this type of instruction. Concise and arranged in a table for easy consultation.

- Yoder, S. (1990). *What's under the hood: How a disk drive works.* Computing Teacher, 18,1, 16–18.
  Gives students a glimpse of hardware operation and information retrieval and storage. Adult learners will appreciate having some of the mystery of computer technology removed for them when they see how the machine works.

Software Guides

- Goulding, P., Tumpane, M. and Watkins, A. (1988). *Teaching methodology, annotated software evaluations and publishers' information, part II.* Toronto, ON: George Brown College.
  As well as being a comprehensive annotated list of software specific to content areas, this manual includes a statement of philosophy and approaches to classroom use. A complete list of publishers is supplied.

- People's Computer. (1989). *Adult literacy and technology guide to literacy software.* San Ramon, CA: Author. (Write to 2682 Bishop Drive, Suite 107, San Ramon, CA 94583.)
  An annotated guide using a description of the product and its strengths and weaknesses. This can be a good start to exploring possible purchases.

- Montana State. (1989). *Computer software for teaching basic skills to adults. An evaluation.* Helena, MT: Montana State Department of Public Instruction. (ERIC Document Reproduction Service No. ED 311 209.)
  Many helpful ideas for selecting appropriate software.

- International Society for Technology in Education. (1989). *Educational software preview guide.* Redwood City, CA: International Society for Technology in Education. (Write to University of Oregon, 1787 Agate Street, Eugene, OR 97403.)

  While there is no annotation or evaluation included, this guide does list many more applications than other manuals. Listings include their use, level and price.

Selected Software Companies[1]

- Hartley Courseware, 133 Bridge Street, Dimondale, MI 48821
- Humanities Software, 19723 S. Katerine Court, Cerritos, CA 97061
- Scholastic Software, 730 Broadway, New York, NY 10003
- Skillsbank, 4718 Hartford Avenue, Baltimore, MD 21214
- Teacher Support Software, P.O. Box 7125, Gainsville, FL 32605.

Integrated Comprehensive Systems[2]

- *PALS, IBM Corp.*, 1133 Westchester Avenue, White Plains, NY 10604; or, in Canada, IBM Canada, 79 Wellington Street West, 6th Floor, Toronto, ON M5K 1B1
- *WICAT,* 1875 South State Street, Orem, UT 84058
- Wasatch Educational Systems, Orem, UT 84058
- *INVEST,* Josten's Learning Corp., 6170 Cornerstone Ct. East, Suite 310, San Diego, CA 92121
- Computer Curriculum Corp., P.O. Box 3711, Sunnyvale, CA 94088.
- Tro/The Roach Corp., 4660 W. 77th Street, Edina, MN 55435.

  (Supplied by Claudia Bredemus, Curriculum Developer for St. Paul School's Adult Literacy and Special Needs Programs in a Symposium at the Adult Literacy and Technology Conference, 18–21 July, 1990.)

---

[1] Additions to those found in Goulding, Tumpane and Watkins, 1988.

[2] These companies sell systems that include audio, visual and print capabilities. It is the total package approach.

4.4 Occupational Literacy

- Askov, E. (1989). *Upgrading Basic Skills for the Workplace.* University Park, PA: Pennsylvania State University, Institute for the Study of Adult Literacy. (ERIC Document Reproduction Service No. ED 309 297.)

  A manual describing how to develop a literacy program for the workplace and how to market it. Includes sample learning activities.

- Auten, A. (1980). *The challenge: Job literacy in the 1980s.* Journal of Reading, 23,8, 750–754.

  One approach to this subject is to assess the reading requirements of a specific job and to present material relevant to that assessment. This article identifies the resources related to that process.

- Bernardon, N.L. (1989). *Let's erase illiteracy from the workplace.* Personnel, 66,1, 29–32.

  (See Section 3.3, "Using Computers.")

- Berney, K. (1988). *Can your workers read?* Nation's Business, (October), 26–28, 30, 32, 34.

  Defines workplace literacy and identifies means for remediating workers' basic skills.

- Butler, E. (1985). *Understanding and guiding the career development of adolescents and young adults with learning disabilities.* Springfield, IL: C.C. Thomas.

  Discusses and demonstrates how the decision-making capabilities around issues of self, family and job are affected in learning-disabled young adults. Uses Super's career development theory which highlights self-concept as a major factor in career selection.

- Carnevale, A.P., Gainer, L.J. and Melzer, A.S. (1988). *Workplace basics: The skills employers want.* Alexandra, VA: American Society for Training and Development, U.S. Department of Labour; Employment and Training Administration. (Write 1630 Duke Street, Box 1443, Alexandra, VA. 22313.)

  Describes a complete list of skills, both academic and interpersonal, that are necessary for success on the job. These have been identified by employers.

- Collino, G.E., Aderman, E.M. and Askov, E.N. (1988). *Literacy and job performance: A perspective.* University Park, PA: The Institute for the Study of Adult Literacy, Penn State University. (Write to 248 Calder Way, Suite 307, University Park, PA 16802.)

  Relates management's view of basic skills training as well as general ideas about literacy in the workplace.

- Chang, K. (1987). *Occupational literacy: An overview.* Lifelong Learning: An Omnibus of Practice and Research, 11,1, 19–22.

  Summarizes the need for research and some things that have been accomplished. One of the latter is the difference between reading demands in school curricula and occupational demands.

- Cornell, T. (1988). *Characteristics of effective occupational literacy programs.* Journal of Reading, 31,6, 654–656.

  An outline of basic program characteristics required for meaningful results. Two of these are: increasing the time working on a task through action learning, and using a competency based system wherein the skills and knowledge needed for the job are assessed and taught.

- Diel, W. and Mikulecky, L. (1988). The nature of reading at work. In Kintgen, E., Kroll, B. and Rose, M. (Eds.). *Perspectives on literacy.* Carbondale and Edwardsville, IL: Southern Illinois University Press.

  A review of the literature and a study specifically designed to observe the role of reading in certain job areas.

- Drew, R.A. and Mikulecky, L. (1988). *How to gather and develop job specific literacy materials for basic skills instruction.* Bloomington, IN: The Office of Education and Training Resources, School of Education, Indiana University. (Write to 840 State Park Road, 46 Bypass, Room 110, Bloomington, IN 47405.)

  Provides a good set of guidelines and questions for compiling a job-related curriculum.

- Gedal, S. (1989). *Between Paulo Freire and Tom Sticht: Adult education and job training at Boston Technical Center.* Connections: A Journal of Adult Literacy, 3, 54–62. (ERIC Document Reproduction Services No. ED 310 289.)

  A case study of a basic skills programs for adults who want to enter a particular job training program. Identifies the tensions between training and adult education.

- Jackson, N. (1987). Skill training in transition: Implications for women. In Gaskell, J. and McLaren, A.T. (Eds.). *Women in education.* Calgary, AB: Detselig Enterprises Limited.

  Discusses the issue of skills training as it relates to the status of women workers.

- Levy, M. (1988). *The role of core skills in work based learning.* Transition from Education Through Employment, (October), 17–19.

  Describes an Employment Thinking program designed to break down tasks and necessary skills and provides techniques for assessing these skills. (Note: This journal may be ordered from Personnel Publications Ltd., 1 Hills Place, London, England W1R 1AG.)

- Mark, J.L. (1987). *Let ABE do it: Basic education in the workplace.* Washington, DC: American Association of Continuing and Adult Education. (Write 1112 16th Street N.W., Suite 420, Washington, DC 20036.)

  Two hundred programs are listed and described from which resources may be obtained.

- Marsick, V. (1987). *Learning in the Workplace.* London, UK: Croom Helm.

  Discusses how to develop both a learning environment and a learning community within an organization that tends to be mechanistic. Reflects on behaviourist paradigm of literacy instruction.

- Mikulecky, L. (1982). *Job literacy: The relationship between school preparation and workplace actuality.* Reading Research Quarterly, 17, 400–419.

  A study of the demands of workplace literacy and whether school prepares students for these demands. Results suggest that workers read more on the job than students, read more difficult material more competently, and with better reading strategies.

- Mikulecky, L. (1984). *Preparing students for workplace literacy demands.* Journal of Reading, 28,3, 253–257.

  Determines that problem solving, use of judgement, and analysis of problem-posing situations are more common on the job than in school.

- Mikulecky, L. and Ehlingher, J. (1986). *The influence of metacognitive aspects of literacy on the job performance of electronic technicians.* Journal of Reading, 18,1, 41–62.

  Data collected to analyze the literacy abilities and on-the-job performance of electronic technicians. The technique could be applied to other job areas.

- Mikulecky, L. and Winchester, D. (1983). *Job literacy and job performance among nurses at varying employment levels.* Adult Education Quarterly, 34,1, 1–15.

  Analyzes job performance for nurses in training, experienced nurses, and supervisory nurses. Suggests that differences reside in their ability to apply critical skills to what is read rather than just the reading of text.

- Miller, L.E. and Feggestad, K. (1987). *Teaching employees to solve problems.* Vocational Education Journal, 62,3, 28–29.

  Uses an eight-step problem-solving process as systematic training for employees. The process includes “determining changes, identifying causes and testing possibilities," important steps in working through a problem on the job.

- Osipow, S. (1969). *Cognitive styles and educational vocational preferences and selection.* Journal of Counselling Psychology, 16,6, 534–546.
  (See Section 1.2, "Learning Styles.")

- Patterson, M. (1989). *Workplace literacy: A review of the literature.* Fredericton, NB: Department of Advanced Education and Training. (ERIC Document Reproduction Service No. ED 314 142.)
  Canadian data suggest that basic skills training is moving from general education to a strict job-related focus. Well referenced.

- Penfield, J. (1984). *Integrating ESL and the workplace.* Highland Park, NJ: Penfield Associates. (Write to P.O. Box 4493, Highland Park, NJ 0894.)
  Describes preparation for entry-level jobs in health services. Using job descriptions, presents vocabulary and skills list to prepare reading materials

- Pershing, J.A. (Ed.). (1988). *Bridging education and employment with basic academic skills.* Bloomington, IN: Indiana University. (See Drew and Mikulecky entry for address.)
  A comprehensive volume which includes a task analysis of the skills required for specific jobs and also relates them to various areas of the curriculum for teaching purposes.

- Philippi, J. (1988). *Matching literacy to job training: Some applications from military programs.* Journal of Reading, 31,7, 658–666.
  Details of an on-the-job program which specifically addresses reading needs, including a description of the process and competencies considered.

- Rayman, J.R. (1981). *Computer-assisted career guidance for adults.* New Directions for Continuing Education, 10, 77–83.
  (See Section 3.3, "Using Computers.")

- Rush, R.T., Moe, A.J. and Storlie, R.L. (1986). *Occupational literacy education.* Newark, DE: International Reading Association.

  A language-oriented approach to on-the-job training with a focus on learning for meaning.

- Terdy, D. (1989). *The "New Market:" Adult literacy and employment in the year 2000.* Illinois School Journal, 68,2, 11–19.

  Suggests that partnerships between business and adult literacy programs could open up rewarding new opportunities for workers. Cooperation in needs assessment and material selection could better suit the needs of the employee and employee.

5

FUTURE DIRECTIONS AND RESOURCES

Future Directions

While there is a great deal of literature dealing with the subject of literacy and adult education, there is surprisingly little written about future directions that should be taken. Several books that review the literacy environment (e.g., de Castell, Luke and Egan, 1986; Kintgen, Kroll and Rose, 1988; Taylor and Draper, 1989) encourage a variety of perspectives including an historical frame of reference. These appear to cover the ground thoroughly; however, they do not venture a focus on the future needs and directions for training in this field. Levine (1986) spent time to discuss the "future of literacy and literacies of the future" (pp. 183–207). He included discussion on the oral-literate transition and the relationship between literacy and the information explosion. In the latter discussion, Levine uses the sheer volume of print information and electronic information networks as determinants of either "a true technology of freedom" or as "determinants of what information is available to whom" (p. 196), depending on how one looks at it. He then asks what impact this new environment will have on traditional literacy skills and on the people who lack them. The relationship between print and electronic information leads to speculation of "future literacies" (in which the computer plays a more significant role) and the education needed to survive within them. He speculates on the social and political perspectives that would impact on these trends.

The following section gives a short list that is representative of what could be culled from researched papers. This paucity of information led us to consider what still needs to be done.

Needs

There is a need to understand and provide:

1. More research into the non-participation in literacy programs. These non-participants tend to be in the 0–8 grade level groups. Of these, many are women. This may mean a restructuring of program delivery systems to deinstitutionalize some programming so that access is easier (Beder, 1990; MacKeracher, 1984; both in the Literacy section).
2. More research into minority groups and their specific learning styles—in particular, native groups, newcomers to Canada, women, the aged, and participants in corrections. Their learning styles may not always fit established norms (cf. Hunter and Harman, 1988, in Literacy section; Taylor and Draper, 1989, in Adult Education section). This should result in a clearer understanding of how teaching methods can be changed to suit specific client groups and to better decide whether integration of specific programs is appropriate or not.
3. A less confounded definition and an understanding of how teachers perceive "meeting learner needs." Currently, it is a theoretical concept. In many instructional settings addressing literacy, learner needs are still being defined by the instructor (Cameron, 1986; Mezirow, 1990, in Adult Education section; Hayes and Valentine, 1989, in Literacy section)
4. Teacher training and in-service professional development that does not centre around data-heavy sessions related to literacy statistics. While they have also included intricate descriptions of successful teaching techniques, most adult educators have not been trained to work specifically with adults. Some techniques may be similar to teaching in other areas (e.g., primary school), but most ways of working with adults are different. We need to allow some scrutiny of methods and approaches actually being used in the classroom to see how they fit into commonly accepted adult education practices (Chall, 1987, Literacy section).

Finally, universities must keep pace with the demands of educators. In this expanding area of lifelong learning, there are few universities in Canada educating and preparing adult educators and designating courses and programs specific to that area.

The pages that follow are designed to provide you, the practitioner, with sources of information, action and advocacy which can assist you in making decisions for future directions for your program. While the "literacy community" may be currently short on visions for the future, resources are in place for any potential. We wish you good luck in your journey.

SOURCES

- Deshler, D. and Hagan, N. (1989). *Adult education research: issues and directions.* In Merriam, S. and Cunningham, P. (Eds.). Handbook of Adult and Continuing Education. San Francisco: Jossey-Bass.

  Starts by comparing the positivist (empirical) and constructivist (naturalist) view of research. Advocates action research which is classroom-based and is a catalyst for change. There is a call for research on workplace learning and on knowledge acquisition, both of which are relevant issues in this bibliography.

- Kazemek, F. (1990). *Adult literacy education: heading into the 1990s.* Adult Education Quarterly, 41,1, 62.

  Six different volumes are considered in a composite review of literacy concerns. Advocates a closer look at the socioeconomics of the country to determine the effect on literacy development among different groups in society. Determines that the "stationary poor" are not being reached by literacy initiatives and that the real purpose of literacy education is not being realized. This is a call for action in which every literacy educator can be involved.

- Parker, J.T. (1990). *Modeling a future for adult basic education.* Adult Learning, 1,4, 16–18.

  Reviewing 25 years of adult basic education, the author identifies four models for the future: service to target populations, programs with an employment focus, professionalization of Adult Basic Education, and widely spread non-intensive efforts.

Literacy Organizations

In Canada

- Canadian Association for Adult Education, 29 Prince Arthur Avenue, Toronto, ON M5R 1B2 (416–964–0559)

  This organization promotes education by linking educators across Canada.

- Canadian Congress for Learning Opportunities for Women, 47 Main Street, Toronto, On M4E 2V6 (416–699–1909)

  A national non-profit organization addressing women's issues related to research in education, advocacy and literacy. Publishing, in the near future, a resource book directing practitioners toward women-positive materials.

- Canadian Organization for Development Through Education, 321 Chapel Street, Ottawa, ON K1N 7Z2 (613–232 3569)

  Strives to improve self-worth in third world countries by sending books and other print materials to libraries and schools.

- Frontier College, 35 Jackes Avenue, Toronto, ON M4T 1E2 (416–923–3591)

  Its mandate is to train volunteer literacy tutors and match them to appropriate learners.

- International Council for Adult Education, 720 Bathurst Street, Room 500, Toronto, ON M5S 2R4 (416–588–1211)

  Supports educators in 98 different countries by providing conferences and workshops all over the world. Centres on the empowerment of working people for the purpose of social change.

- Laubach Literacy Council, Box 2246, Station B, Kitchener, ON N2H 6M2 (519–741–0900)

  Teaches basic reading and writing skills to adults using phonetically based materials. Students pay only for their books. Instruction is free. Speakers available. Many major and medium-sized cities support their own councils. Consult the Directory of Associations in Canada available at the library for further help.

Literacy Access

- Metro Toronto Region (1–416–961–5557)

  This is an information referral source. It covers areas as far west as Pickering and out to Halton, Ontario, but it can often help you with other concerns.

- Movement for Canadian Literacy, 880 Wellington Street, Suite 701, Ottawa, ON K1R 6K7 (613–563–2464)

  A national, non-profit agency whose main interest is public awareness. It links individuals with organizations that can fulfil their educational needs. Advocates with the government also.

- National Literacy Database (NALD), Fanshawe College, 1460, Oxford Street East, London, ON N5W 5H1 (519–452–4446)

  This is a complete database of community college programs and services available in Canada. Developed for the Association of Canadian Community Colleges, this database is available through INET and in print form and is regularly updated. An invaluable source of college-based information.

- Ontario Association for Adult Education, 8 York Street, 7th Floor, Toronto, ON M5J 1R2 (416–366–2374)

  Interested in all aspects of program delivery.

- Ontario Literacy Coalition, 365 Bloor Street East, Suite 1003, Toronto, ON M4W 3M7 (416–963–5787)

  A provincial literacy network linking up school boards, colleges and community programs. Advocacy is their main issue.

- Ontario Native Literacy Coalition, 787-2nd Avenue, Owen Sound, ON N4K 2G9 (519 371-5594).

  Tutor training information, promotion, and fund-raising are provided.

- Parkdale (Ontario) Project READ, 1303 Queen Street West, Toronto, ON M6K 1L6 (416–531–6308)

  Trains tutors and arranges classes in literacy.

- Toronto Adult Literacy for Action Centre, 1900 Davenport Road, Toronto, ON M6N 4Y2 (416–652–3652)

  Formerly West End Literacy, this centre deals with community issues in adult literacy and advocates on behalf of the community.

- Workers' Educational Association of Canada, 736 Bathurst Street, Toronto, ON M5S 2R4 (416–588–6323)
  A referral association for literacy education to suggest where programs in adult education can be accessed.

- World Literacy of Canada, 692 Coxwell Avenue, Toronto, ON M4L 3B6 (416–465–4667)
  Responsible for publishing a worldwide newsletter for policy makers and program planners.

In the United States

- Action/Vista Literacy Corps, 806 Connecticut Avenue NW Washington, DC 20525
  Volunteers in Service to America Literacy Corps develops programs to address literacy needs, heighten public awareness, and combat illiteracy. (*Literacy Forum Resource Package: A Resource Handbook* (1983) may be useful.)

- Adult Learning Association, Star Route, Waterville, WA 98858
  Publishes *Adult Basic Education* magazine and *Adult Learner* and consults with tutors, counsellors, libraries and others in need of adult basic education information. Provides information on teaching methods, funding and recruitment.

- Adult Literacy and Technology Project, 203 Rackley Building, University Park, PA 16802
  Related to researching and promoting the integration of technology into adult literacy and basic education practices; publishes newsletter, LitLine bulletin board; Conference proceedings from June 1987.

- Adult Literacy Initiative (ALI), U.S. Department of Education, 400 Maryland Avenue SW, Washington, DC 20202
  A government agency providing on-line support and funding for all types of literacy initiatives. Active in public awareness issues.

- American Association for Adult and Continuing Education, 1201 16th Street NW, Suite 230, Washington, DC 20036
  A professional organization providing leadership and encouraging research among educators in adult education.

Publishes *Lifelong Learning* and *Adult Education Quarterly* as well as a variety of resource publications, pamphlets, books and monographs.

- Assault on Illiteracy Program, 410 Central Park West, PH-C, New York, NY 10025

  Works with a network of organizations aimed at alleviating illiteracy in the black community.

- Association for Community-Based Education, 1806 Vernon Street NW, Washington, DC 20009

  A national association working on job counselling, career preparation, and basic skills instruction in community programs. Information on funding and advocacy techniques are available as well as a publication *Adult Literacy: Study of Community-Based Literacy Programs* (1986). An annual conference is held.

- Business Council for Effective Literacy Inc., 1221 Avenue of the Americas, New York, NY 10020

  Fosters greater corporate awareness of adult functional illiteracy and increasing business involvement in the literacy field. The BCEL Bulletin is a how-to guide for business literacy programs and another newsletter addresses literacy research and practice.

- Clearinghouse on Adult Education, U.S. Department of Education, Room 522, Reporters Building, 400 Maryland Avenue SW, Washington, DC 20202–5515

  Has published *What Works in Adult Literacy* and *Promising Practices in Workplace Literacy* as well as other materials related to adult education. Bibliographies and resource guides are also available.

- Educational Resources Information Centre (ERIC),
  (1) Clearinghouse on Adult, Career, and Vocational Education, Ohio State University, 1960 Kennedy Road, Columbus OH 43210–1090
  (2) Clearinghouse on Reading and Communications Skills, 1111 Kenyon Road, Urbana IL 61801

  Both Centres provide information on accessing the database, submitting documents, and obtaining materials. Packaged searches on high-interest topics and other journal articles are available.

- Institute for the Study of Adult Literacy, Pennsylvania State University, College of Education, 301 Rackley Building, University Park, PA 16802
  Covers all aspects of literacy involvement, including research, the use of technology and media in adult literacy, staff development, and the compilation of materials for planning.

- Literacy Volunteers of America Inc., 404 Oak Street, Syracuse, NY 13203
  Publishes a variety of training and program management materials, including workbooks, videos and audiotapes to agencies providing ongoing support to nonprofessional volunteer tutors. A catalogue lists reading materials in the Adult Literacy Series.

- World Education Inc., 210 Lincoln Street, Boston, MA 02111
  A private organization providing training and technical assistance in nonformal education for adults. Currently developing a master's-level program in literacy at the University of Massachusetts to provide summer training in curricula relevant to basic education. Publishes *Focus on Basics*, a resource bulletin for teachers in basic skills training with adults.

Useful Journals, Newsletters and Periodicals

- *Academic Therapy*, PRO-ED Journals, 8700 Shoal Creek Boulevard, Austin, TX 78758–6897
  Published five times yearly, it deals with special and remedial education issues of an interdisciplinary nature.

- *Adult Literacy and Basic Education*, Kellogg Centre, Montana State University, Bozeman, MT 59717
  Published three times a year, this journal includes social and pedagogical issues in the field of literacy.

- *Adult Education Quarterly*, Department of Adult Education, 422 Tucker Hall, University of Georgia, Athens, GA 30602
  Reviews research, philosophy and theoretical issues.

- *Business Council for Effective Literacy,* 1221 Avenue of the Americas, 35th Floor, New York, NY 10020

  A quarterly newsletter for business people and literacy practitioners.

- *Canadian Journal for the Study of Adult Education,* Canadian Association for the Study of Adult Education, Dr. D.H. Bundage, Department of Adult Education, Ontario Institute for Studies in Education, 252 Bloor Street West, Toronto, ON M5S 1V6

  Accepts papers on enquiry into the field at all levels.

- *Canadian Journal of Education,* Canadian Society for the Study of Education, 14 Henderson Avenue, Ottawa, ON K1N 7P1

  Published quarterly, it includes research reports, theoretical papers and critical reviews in all areas of education.

- *Classroom Computer Learning,* 2451 East River Road, Dayton, OH 45439

  A newsletter with a distinct focus on educational issues.

- *Computers in Education,* Moorshead Publications Limited, 1300 Don Mills Road, Toronto. M3B 3M8

  Published 10 times yearly, it deals with hardware and software for educational purposes for the experienced user only.

- *Computing Teacher,* International Society for Technology in Education, University of Oregon, 1787 Agate Street, Eugene, OR 97403–9905

  Published eight times over ten months, it addresses the instructional uses of computers at the pre-college level.

- *Convergence,* International Council for Adult Education, 720 Bathurst Street, Toronto, ON M5S 2R4

  Produced quarterly, it debates literacy issues from a worldwide perspective.

- *Harvard Educational Review,* Gutman Library, Suite 349, 6 Appian Way, Cambridge, MA 02138–3752

  Published quarterly, it reflects contemporary issues of a general nature.

- *International Journal of Lifelong Education,* Taylor & Francis Limited, 4 John Street, London, England WC1N 2ET

  Published quarterly, this journal reflects concerns in continuing education worldwide.

- *Journal of Computer-Based Instruction,* Association for the Development of Computer-Based Instructional Systems, Miller Hall 409, Western Washington University, Bellingham, WA 98225

  Published quarterly, this journal examines general theoretical and practical considerations.

- *Journal of Reading,* International Reading Association, 800 Barksdale Road, P.O. Box 8139, Newark, DE 19714–8139

  Reflects current theoretical research and practice in all levels of education in eight yearly publications.

- *Learning Styles Network Newsletter,* Centre for the Study of Learning and Teaching Styles, St. John's University, Utopia Parkway, Jamaica, NY 11439

  Short but interesting articles on the use of learning style identification in a number of contexts—school, college and the workplace.

- *Lifelong Learning: An Omnibus of Practise and Research,* American Association for Adult and Continuing Education, 1112 16th Street NW, Suite 420, Washington, DC 20036

  Published eight times annually, it contains many articles relevant to adults. (Note: Recently replaced by *Adult Learning.*)

- *Lifelong Learning in Ontario,* Ontario Association for Continuing Education, 736 Bathurst Street, Unit 11, Toronto, ON M5S 2R4

  A newsletter designed to report activities in adult education.

- *Literacy on the Move.* (See Ontario Literacy Coalition—Organizations in Canada.)

- *Reading Horizons,* Reading Center and Clinic, Western Michigan University, Kalamazoo, MI 49008

  Published quarterly, it is devoted to teaching reading at all levels.

- *Reading Research Quarterly,* International Reading Association, 800 Barksdale Road, P.O. Box 8139, Newark, DE 19714–8139

  Published quarterly to reflect theory, research and practice in reading.

- *Studies in the Education of Adults,* National Institute of Adult Continuing Education, 19B De Montfort Street, Leicester, England LE1 7GE

  Published bi-annually, it includes work on theoretical, empirical and historical issues.

- *Window on Technology,* Ministry of Community and Social Services, Program Technology Branch, 12th Floor - 5140 Yonge Street, Toronto, ON M2N 6L7

  At present published quarterly, this newsletter supplies those working in human services programs with news of the aids and devices for disabled learners.

Publishers (of literacy-related materials)

- ABC-CLIO Inc.
  Santa Barbara, CA 93103

- Action Read Family Literacy
  5 Douglas Street
  Guelph, ON N1H 2S8
  (1–519–836–2759)

- Allyn & Bacon
  1870 Birchmount Road
  Scarborough, ON M1P 2J7

- Cambridge University Press
  The Pitt Building, Trumpington Street
  Cambridge, England CB2 1RP
  or
  32 East 57th Street
  New York, NY 10022

- Curriculum Associates, Inc.
  5 Esquire Road, N. Billerica, MA 01862–2589

- Dominie Press Limited
  345 Nuggett Avenue, Unit 15
  Scarborough, ON M1K 4J4

- Educational Resources Limited, (Includes Steck-Vaughan Co.)
  #109–8475 Ontario Street
  Vancouver, BC V5X 3E8

- Fitzhenry & Whiteside
  195 Allstate Parkway
  Markham, ON L3R 4T8

- Globe/Modern Curriculum Press
  3771 Victoria Park Avenue
  Scarborough, ON M1W 2P9

- International Reading Association
  800 Barksdale Road, P.O. Box 8139
  Newark, DE 19814

- Kilbride Educational Services
  Kilbride, ON L0P 1G0

- Lingui Systems Inc.
  3100 4th Avenue
  East Moline, IL 61244

- Literacy on the Move
  Ontario Literacy Coalition
  365 Bloor Street East, Suite 1003
  Toronto, ON M4W 3M7

- McClelland & Stewart Inc.
  481 University Avenue
  Toronto, ON M5G 2E9

- Monarch Books of Canada
  5000 Dufferin Street, Unit K
  Downsview, ON M3H 5T5
  (also handles Heinemann publications)

- National Textbook Company
  A Division of NTC Publishing Group
  4255 West Touhy Avenue
  Lincolnwood (Chicago), IL 60646–1975

- Niagara Regional Literacy Council
  57 Facer Street
  St. Catharines, ON L2M 5H9

- Penguin Books Canada Limited
  2801 John Street
  Markham, ON L3R 1B4

- Personnel Publications Ltd.
  1 Hills Place
  London, England W1R 1AG

- Pippin Publishing Limited
  1361 Huntingwood Drive, Unit 7
  Agincourt, ON M1S 3J1

- OISE Publishing
  252 Bloor Street West
  Toronto, ON M5S 1V5

- Prentice Hall, Simon and Schuster
  Englewood Cliffs, NJ 07632

- Rumours Games
  P.O. Box 4253, Station C
  London, ON N5W 5J6

- SOI Systems, A Division of M & M Systems
  45755 Goodpasture Road
  Vida, OR 97488

- Steck-Vaughan Company
  (see Educational Resources)

- Teachers' College Press
  1234 Amsterdam Avenue
  New York, NY 10027

- Teacher Support Software
  P.O. Box 7130
  Gainesville, FL 32605

- Thompson Educational Publishing, Inc
  11 Briarcroft Road,
  Toronto, ON M6S 1H3

- United States Department of Education
  Clearinghouse on Adult Education and
  Literacy Division of Adult Education and Literacy
  Washington, DC 20202–7240